PERSONAL EVANGELISM

How to lead people to Christ
Helping people follow Christ

COART RAMEY

Bob Jones University Press, Greenville, South Carolina 29614

This textbook was written by members of the faculty and staff of Bob Jones University. Standing for the "old-time religion" and the absolute authority of the Bible since 1927, Bob Jones University is the world's leading Fundamentalist Christian university. The staff of the University is devoted to educating Christian men and women to be servants of Jesus Christ in all walks of life.

Providing unparalleled academic excellence, Bob Jones University prepares its students through its offering of over one hundred majors, while its fervent spiritual emphasis prepares their minds and hearts for service and devotion to the Lord Jesus Christ.

If you would like more information about the spiritual and academic opportunities available at Bob Jones University, please call
1-800-BJ-AND-ME (1-800-252-6363).
www.bju.edu

NOTE:
The fact that materials produced by other publishers are referred to in this volume does not constitute an endorsement by Bob Jones University Press of the content or theological position of materials produced by such publishers. The position of Bob Jones University Press, and the University itself, is well known. Any references and ancillary materials are listed as an aid to the student or the teacher and in an attempt to maintain the accepted academic standards of the publishing industry.

PERSONAL EVANGELISM AND DISCIPLESHIP

Coart Ramey, M.A.

Editor: V. Edward Myers, M. Div.
Cover: Ellyson Kalagayan
Compositor: Carol Anne Ingalls

©1999 Bob Jones University Press
Greenville, South Carolina 29614

Printed in the United States of America
All rights reserved

ISBN 1-57924-312-6

15   14   13   12   11   10   9   8   7   6   5   4   3   2

CONTENTS

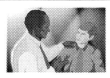

To the Teacher

Goals

When we designed this course, we had the following goals in mind:

1. Present personal evangelism and personal discipleship as one integrated process called disciple making. Too often, either part of the process is studied in isolation from the other. In keeping with the Great Commission and the principles in the book of Acts, this course attempts to teach evangelism and discipleship as a unity.

2. Establish a firm doctrinal basis for personal disciple making. Theology cannot be separated from practical methods of ministry. What the Bible teaches about the nature of man, sin, and salvation determines the practice by which we seek to make disciples for Christ.

3. Explain an effective procedure for personal evangelism and equip the students to practice it during the course. A flexible model for soul-winning guides the students to establish contact with people they do not already know in order to proclaim the gospel to them. Class projects require the students to pass out tracts, report on a soul-winning encounter, and lead a person through a practice discipleship course.

Introduction

The small group of plainly dressed men watched politely as one of their number stepped behind the rough wooden pulpit. He announced the topic of his sermon in that simple, calm manner he always used when preaching. The title, "An Inquiry into the Obligation of Christians to Use Means for the Conversion of the Heathen," piqued the audience's interest. It implied that William thought Christian people should be taking it upon themselves to teach the heathen about God!

That truly was a surprising message from a preacher in William's day. Good Christian people of that period believed that God would convert the "heathen" whenever He pleased. Did the Bible not teach as much? While pouring much time and thought into studying his Bible, William had realized that God says *Christians* are to tell unsaved people about Christ without waiting for a special sign or event. God has issued standing orders to all His people to tell the heathen about Jesus Christ.

William, whose last name was Carey, became the first figure in a tide of British missionaries that spread around the world during the next 150 years. Why was telling unsaved people about Christ such a novel thought until William's sermon? People in earlier centuries had shared the gospel freely. The problem in William Carey's eighteenth-century England was that virtually everyone called himself a Christian. Everyone knew what a Christian was. If you would have asked a woman on the street if she were trusting Jesus Christ for salvation, she would have certainly replied "yes," and probably been irritated that you even asked.

It is not that the British were all truly saved the Bible way; on the contrary, many did not really understand the gospel. They called themselves Christian whether or not they were genuinely saved.

In a society of nominal Christians, the true Christians find it difficult to keep telling others about Christ. The gospel seems like old news. It is much easier to carry on the routine Christian life without deliberately evangelizing unsaved people.

But no one even claimed to be a Christian in India, the place where Carey wanted to evangelize the lost. By studying his Bible,

William Carey

William Carey was a remarkable man who taught himself several languages while working at his trade, mending shoes. He became a missionary when no one knew what a missionary should do. Despite sickness, persecution, and his wife's mental illness, he stayed on the mission field over forty years. He is a tremendous testimony of God's ability to show supernatural strength through a mortal man's weakness.

The sermon mentioned in the student text was delivered at Clipstone in Leicester, England, in 1791. Carey lived out his sermon by serving as a missionary for forty years, primarily in Serampore, India. He saw relatively little fruit in relation to the time invested but made an enduring contribution to future missions by translating the Bible into several Indian languages. The task required mastering not only the original languages of the Bible (Greek and Hebrew) but also the different languages into which he translated the Word of God. He learned each of these Indian dialects as an adult. Probably the best biography of William Carey is by S. Pearce Carey.

Project One

Tell the students to pass out ten tracts to ten different people. If possible, use ten different tracts. Before passing out the tracts, the students should read through each tract carefully, evaluating its strengths and weaknesses. Think about what types of people might respond best to each tract.

In class, have your students read each tract and rate it according to visual appeal, clarity, use of Scripture, and length. Note different characteristics of the tracts. Tracts often fall into one of the following categories: step by step gospel tracts, eternal punishment tracts, special occasion tracts, story tracts, personal testimony tracts, celebrity tracts, controversial issue tracts, and survey tracts.

Students should give each tract to a different person, preferably a stranger. With your permission, a student may give one to an unsaved person he already knows. Have students give an oral or written report (three sentences) of what happened with each tract, including who received the tract, where the tract was given out, and how the recipient responded.

Offer some ideas on how to pass out the tracts. Students may give them to store clerks, neighbors, or persons met during door-to-door visitation. You may be able to take a class outing to a local park or shopping mall. Ideally, a

William Carey realized God wants His people to take the gospel to the heathen—people who have never heard it. God's will for English Christians had been the same in the years before Carey lived, but few had understood and obeyed it as Carey did.

Are the people in your area Christians, nominal Christians, or heathens? True Christians are rarely a majority. What percentage of teenagers and adults go to a church, any church, on Sunday mornings? How many of those churches teach the gospel as the Bible teaches it? Most of the people in your neighborhood and town are probably a mixture of nominal Christians and heathens who would not even claim Christianity.

So why bother being a Christian? After all, if it is not popular to be a *real* Christian, why even go to the trouble? Real Christians obey the Bible, and the Bible says Christians are supposed to tell other people how to become Christians. All those people in your town are happy remaining as they are. They do not need you to tell them how to be happy or go to heaven. You will do them more good by just showing what a good person you are and by having a positive influence on society.

Right?

If no one has ever said those words to you, just wait; someone will. Most nominal Christians believe those ideas are true. naturally, nominal Christians call themselves real Christians. They think reasoning and common sense show that Christians have no business trying to evangelize those who do not want to be evangelized. Consequently, they slide unknowingly toward the kind of culture in which William Carey lived in England, a culture in which everyone assumes everyone else either is a Christian or would become one if he cared to.

student could give one tract to the stranger he involves in project two.

Assignment: Design and write a tract of your own. You could assign this project immediately after completing Chapter 1. This assignment would also make a good group project. Students should use blank paper, though it may be colored paper. They may design the tract on full-size paper but must specify the actual dimensions of the tract. Students may want to produce a pro-

fessional looking tract using a computer.

Sketch in any artwork, draw boxes with descriptions for any photos, and write the text just as it would appear on the final product.

Encourage creative and artistic variety, but focus on the need to communicate the gospel in a concise, effective manner.

Project Two

Witness to the same unsaved person at least twice during the time of the course. The goal is to teach students to establish open witnessing relationships with people they do not know well. They should not use a relative or familiar acquaintance.

One way to accomplish this goal is to visit a stranger, share your personal testimony, leave a tract, and return to

What are your own feelings about sharing the gospel of Jesus Christ with others? If you honestly have no desire to tell others what Christ has done to save them, please carefully consider your own relationship with Him. When you recognize the plain facts of what the Lord Jesus did for you to save you from your sin, you ought to at least acknowledge your debt to Him. What is more, if you have trusted the Lord to save you, you and He are now friends. As His friend, you should be steadily learning more about Him and how you can please Him.

So how does pleasing Christ relate to telling other people about Him? You say, "Because Christ is pleased when I tell people about Him. Sure, sure. I've heard that one plenty of times." But why is He so pleased when you share the gospel? God is pleased because he sees it as a sacrifice from a loving heart. If you love the Lord, it is only natural to want to tell other people about Him. The problem is that witnessing is *hard!*

William Carey pioneered the Baptist Missionary Society in 1792.

talk about the tract a few days later. If an unsaved person agrees to go through the discipleship booklet for project three, the student can fulfill project three at the same time.

Have each student write a one-paragraph report after his second witnessing opportunity. Even if a student fails to gain a second chance to witness from any contact he makes during the entire course, he should report how he attempted to do so.

Project Three

Practice discipling someone with the enclosed *Basics for Believers*. The student needs someone who will commit to sitting and listening cooperatively through five or six sessions. This does not need to be a genuine discipleship situation. The person discipled can be a mature Christian. Depending on the character of your class, you may want to prohibit using family members or classmates.

The student disciple maker and his "disciple" should meet for about half an hour per session. Sessions ought to be at least a day apart, if not several days apart. Pretend the disciple is a new convert who needs every basic doctrine explained in the clearest terms possible. The students may do the first two discipleship lessons before reaching chapter three in the text. Each student needs to do at least five studies with his partner.

William Carey had no idea what difficulties would confront him. He knew what was right, and he knew what God specifically wanted him to do. But the price he eventually paid to be a missionary to India was higher than he could have guessed—the work was very slow, he was often sick, and his wife became mentally ill. The small group of pastors that had gathered to listen to his sermon were the first ones to give money to support Carey's endeavor. They were very poor men. It took great sacrifice for them to send one family around the world. In India, the gospel was not a welcome message. Carey endured many hardships during his years there. Many of the Indians for whom he had given up so much to help wanted nothing to do with Jesus Christ.

Was William Carey right? Why is it necessary to put forth so much time and effort to evangelize the lost? If it were *easy,* you would happily choose to evangelize whenever the opportunity arose. But since it is contrary to your own sinful nature and offensive to every human's inherent sin and pride, evangelizing is (and always will be) *difficult.* Going to the trouble and expense to do what is difficult shows our love for Christ much more than doing an easy task.

The question we have to answer is, "Why is it difficult to turn lost people to Christ?" In answering this question, we will learn why so many people who say they are Christians are not, why evangelism costs so much time and money, and why you find it so much easier not to tell others about Christ.

William Carey became a great missionary, one who left his home country to spread the gospel in another country. This is not a book about missionaries, but it is about the work they and all Christians must do to make other people good disciples of the Lord Jesus Christ.

A *disciple* is a follower, a student who becomes like his master. As a Christian, you are Christ's disciple, and your lifetime task is to make more disciples for Him. Making disciples is the best way to show Him your gratitude—and it is the greatest service you can render another human being!

To provide accountability, you may have the disciple report to you regarding how effectively his discipler taught him the lessons. Have each discipler turn in a written statement that he did the project just as you instructed.

In preparation for the assignment, you may have some students demonstrate a discipleship session in class. Or you may choose a student to be a disciple while you demonstrate how to be a discipler.

Assignment:

When the students reach the sections on personal discipleship in Chapters 4 and 5, they will be taught to show new converts the need for practicing daily devotions and maintaining a prayer journal. These are very good disciplines to build in a new convert or immature Christian. Therefore, your students need to know exactly what it is like to maintain a habit of Bible reading and prayer.

To accomplish this goal, take a class period early in the course to explain the section *A Plan for a Daily Quiet Time with God* on pages 67-69 and the section *Personal Prayer Journal* on page 71. Instruct your class to follow the guidelines laid out for the "4M method" and "ACT" procedure for at least four weeks. As your students follow these methods, they will be prepared to train a "disciple" in personal prayer and Bible study.

CHAPTER ONE

Turning a Rebel into a Disciple

①

Memory Verses: Matthew 28:18-20

Introduction

This course is about the part you play as a Christian in turning a sinner into a faithful child of God. The Lord is working actively throughout the world, drawing people to trust Christ and then grow as Christians. He has you act as His messenger. The message He sends through you is the entire Bible—telling people both how to be saved (the gospel) and what to do after being saved.

Thus there are two halves to your part in turning sinners into disciples:

- telling them how to be saved

- teaching them what God expects of a saved person

Consequently, there are two errors to avoid:

- considering your responsibility completed after leading someone to the Lord

- waiting passively for people to get saved on their own and then come to you to learn about the Bible

Instead, we must envision bringing unsaved people all the way from being rebels against God to being fruitful, joyful children of God. In this first chapter, we want to learn why sin makes discipleship difficult, how Christ wants us to make sinners into disciples, and what will happen to them if we do not.

1

Overview

In this opening chapter we will establish the foundational beliefs of a biblical disciple maker. Certain preliminary facts need to be settled in a Christian's mind in order for him to understand what disciple making is and why he engages in it. Your students must know the truth about human sin, the penalty of rejecting the gospel, and the method and goal of the Lord's Great Commission.

Since this course presents disciple making as a single process integrating evangelism and discipleship, approach the first chapter as the basis for both. When first witnessing to someone, a Christian must know that sin blinds a lost person to the truth and keeps the lost soul from believing the gospel. The Christian must also understand what will happen to the sinner who never trusts Christ. Finally, the Christian must be aware of the Lord's plan for bringing the sinner to salvation. Since God's plan is to forgive that

The Doctrine of Sin

Exercise

Goal: Inductively determine what sin really is.

The following data show the basic nature of sin throughout the Old Testament. Fundamentally, sin means to go in any way other than God's way (Isaiah 53:6). We want to impress upon the students that the people they witness to are not usually going to be

miserable people who are sitting around waiting for someone to tell them how to have a wonderful life. Even if you meet someone in that condition, he normally does not want the true gospel. Instead, people want a way to escape from the burdens of life or from the guilt of their sin.

Most unsaved people believe themselves to be right before God and safe for eternity. Your students will be confronting these people for their whole

lives with a message that is very offensive to human nature. Being told that nothing one does is pleasing to God is a difficult pill for human pride to swallow, especially for a "morally upright" person!

Each student must know as he shares the gospel with a sinner that the soul of a lost person is blind to the truth. The unsaved individual is both ignorant of his own sinful nature and satisfied with himself as he is. Humans do

What Sin Really Is

Let's look at the first chapter of Ezekiel. When you approach someone to tell him about Christ, you will be doing what God's children have done plenty of times before. Ezekiel lived in a time in which many people claimed to serve God but did not obey His Word.

Ezekiel was a Jew, one of God's chosen race. God gave the Jews a country of their own. Through repeated rebellion against God's law and rejection of His prophets, the Jews brought punishment on themselves and lost their country. God allowed another very evil nation, Babylon, to conquer and rule over the Jews.

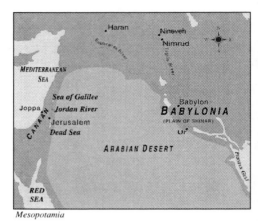

Mesopotamia

Though in exile from the land God gave them, the Jews still would not repent of their sin but continued in rebellion against the Lord. God called Ezekiel to be yet another prophet proclaiming His warning to the people.

Read the first four verses of Ezekiel. Chapter 1 contains Ezekiel's description of his vision of the throne of God in heaven. He saw things that sound strange to us: multifaced, winged creatures; colossal chariot wheels; and the figure of God on His throne. Ezekiel was struggling to put heavenly things into earthly words. God let him see for a few moments heavenly realities. The wheels and living creatures are God's angelic servants; their shapes and forms help display that God's presence and power are spread across the whole earth. The vision was not for Ezekiel's entertainment; it was the basis for what God was about to tell Ezekiel to do.

Put yourself in Ezekiel's sandals as he hears the Lord's command. You told the Lord years ago you would do whatever He wanted, but now that His order has come, you wonder what

2

---

person and then progressively make the person as much like Christ as possible (Ephesians 4:11-16), the Christian should view each person he contacts during soulwinning as someone who has the potential, once saved, to become like Christ. Every discipling relationship is a friendship by which a Christian helps another person to become like Christ.

In a discipling relationship, the mature Christian has to know all about sin in order to help the new Christian eliminate habitual sins from his life. Furthermore, a major goal for any new Christian is to become a disciple maker in his own right; thus, the disciple maker must be ready to teach the disciple all the foundational truths in this first chapter.

Jesus is Jehovah

The person speaking to Ezekiel was Jehovah, the Lord. In order to connect Ezekiel's commission with the Great Commission, show your class that Jesus is Jehovah. John 12:41 records that Isaiah (Esaias) "saw his glory, and spake of him." We can tell from the context in verses 36-42 that Jesus is the "him" in question. The quotations from Isaiah are from chapter 6 in which the prophet saw a vision of the glory of the Lord filling the temple and called the majestic person in the vision "the LORD," or Jehovah. The same title is used to refer to the majestic person who spoke to Ezekiel. Just as Jehovah appeared to Ezekiel to command the prophet to witness, so Jehovah has appeared in the flesh (as Jesus, Jehovah incarnate) to command us to witness.

---

not naturally embrace God; they hate Him and flee from Him. Thus, witnessing for Christ is a struggle against human nature that takes much time and energy and is impossible apart from the miraculous power of God's Holy Spirit.

The fact that effective evangelism requires the Holy Spirit's power brings us to a final, vital point—when you actually see someone accept Christ, it is a miracle. None of man's devices or

methods lead to salvation. We work to do everything exactly God's way, but even when we succeed, God still gets all the credit for every sinner who is born again. You can do everything right and still see no fruit, or you can make mistakes and still see God work miracles!

Direct the following word study exercise to determine what sin is according to the Bible. There are three main root words for sin. Have students look up

and read the references under each of the following words. The students should be able to tell you which word is the one sometimes used for "sin."

Explain to the class that these passages will demonstrate that the Hebrews attached a broader meaning to the idea of sin than we do today. To us, the English word *sin* is a special word with only a religious meaning. In the Old Testament, disobedience to God was a broad concept that was expressed

you've gotten yourself into. Not that you really had a choice; as He is about to demonstrate, God rules all men whether they willingly submit to Him or not!

Read chapter 2:3-5. Notice that there is one phrase to describe Israel and two verbs to define the nation's actions. The phrase is *a rebellious nation*. One verb is *hath rebelled* and the other is *have transgressed*. Was the problem that the people did not know God? The problem was not ignorance but rebellion. **Rebellion** is a willful refusal to obey authority. The Israelites had received more knowledge about God than any other people in history, but despite all they knew about God, they refused to believe it and act on it. Like the nominal Christians in William Carey's England, all of them claimed to follow the true God, but few cared what His Word really said.

The people of Israel not only refused to obey God but were actively disobeying Him. It is not possible to be neutral. Either we do what God commands, or we do what He forbids. The people of Israel "have transgressed," says the Lord in verse 3. **Transgression** is going out of set bounds; it is moving into an off-limits area. Its most basic meaning is leaving a road to wander off into a field. Crossing out of bounds when dribbling a basketball is the same idea. When God uses the word in a moral context, as in Ezekiel 2, the real meaning of sin shows itself. *Sin is rebellion and transgression.* A sinner refuses to do what God says (rebellion) and automatically does what God forbids (transgression).

Tues ↓

What is the attitude of people you know who say they are Christians but act like unsaved people? How do they react when you show them that genuine Christians have lives changed by the truth? They probably act as the Jews did. Look at the two descriptions of them in verse 4: *impudent children* and *stiffhearted*. *Impudence* is an offensive boldness, like a child who stares you in the eye and dares you to spank him.

Ezekiel's Background
Ezekiel as a priest would have begun his ministry in the temple at age 30 (Numbers 4). The thirty years in Ezekiel 1:1 may well refer to the prophet's age when he saw the first vision. Having prepared all his life to take part in the temple ministry, Ezekiel, who became a prisoner in Babylon, was unable to do so. Just when it seemed to be impossible to serve God as Ezekiel had always expected, God called the prophet to a much greater ministry.

An Obedient Witness
Ezekiel did not have a choice about preaching God's Word in the sense that God did not give him any other options. The prophet had a choice in that he could have rebelled against God and refused to do what God commanded. The same is true for your students as they seek God's will for their lives. They will face temptations even now to reject God's leading and to follow their own paths. They need to purpose now not to refuse to do what God wants.

---

with several words having ordinary meanings. A parallel to the Hebrew concept can be found in the English verb "rebel," which is more than a religious word but can be used correctly to describe sin against God.

This word study is based on the following source:

Ronald Youngblood, "A New Look at Three Old Testament Roots for 'Sin.'" *Biblical and Near Eastern Studies* ed. Gary A. Tuttle (Grand Rapids: Eerdmans, 1978) 201-205.

Here are the three words with some basic information. (Your students do not need to understand the details about verb forms and nominals, but the information is provided to use as you see fit.) Take your class through the references under each word, explaining that each group uses the same Hebrew word, even though the English words may differ. Lead the class members to see the basic meanings of each word as given below.

1. *chata'*—Occurs 237 times in 4 verb stems and 354 times as nominals for a total of 591 times. Means basically "miss the road" (Psalm 25:8*b*; Proverbs 8:32, 36 and 19:2). In Kings, it is often associated with not walking in the right way.

2. *ëawa*—Has 17 verb forms and occurs 230 times as nominals,

A Unified Heart

The heart is often called the intellect, emotion, and will. These aspects of the inner man are distinguishable but not divisible.

Stiff here is from a word that means strong or hard, able to resist and defeat opposition, like the strength of a wrestler or the strength of an army. The *heart* is what we often call the mind, the inner person encompassing our thinking, feeling, and decision making. A person with a stiff heart, then, *refuses to agree that he is wrong, refuses to feel any remorse or guilt, and refuses to change his actions.*

Did God assure Ezekiel of results? Verse 5 contains the conditional phrase "Whether . . . or . . ."; God does not promise the preacher that people will believe what he says. He says only that they will eventually know that they have heard the truth! Although the Lord knows in advance how people will respond to His message, He does not tell His messengers what the response will be. When you say to someone, "God is real and living, and He wants you to stop sinning and personally trust Him for your salvation," do you expect that person to instantly drop to his knees in sorrowful repentance?

Read verses 6 and 7 to see what Ezekiel could expect. Does it sound like a fun life? Notice especially the two things Ezekiel was not to fear. When you present the truth to people who are content in their sin, you are guaranteed to get two things: *tough looks* and *sharp words.* Imagine the look that says, "When you grow up, you'll realize life isn't so simple." Or imagine a teen who looks at you as if you were a Martian. Like it or not, looks from others do have a powerful effect on us. It takes real courage to tell a man the truth when the truth hurts.

Worse than tough looks are sharp words. The cliché about sticks and stones breaking what words cannot is deceptive. At your age, you know full well that words strike home in a way punches never do. People may mock you, belittle you, or humiliate you when you try to do them the biggest favor of their lives. God Almighty told Ezekiel to get ready for it.

4

---

totaling 247 times. Means basically "err from the road" (II Samuel 22:24; Isaiah 57:17; Jeremiah 14:10; and Lamentations 3:9).

3. *pasaë*—Has 41 verb forms and 93 nominals for a total of 134 appearances. Means basically "transgress, rebel" (Isaiah 59:13, 15; Amos 2:4; and Hosea 7:13).

The third word *pasaë (psë),* like the first two, frequently occurs in the context of taking a right road over a wrong road. The point is that all three together "show that the transgression/rebellion ingredient in *psë* is often that of willful deviation from the road of godly living, and that *psë* therefore takes its place alongside *ht'* [chata'] and *ëwy* [ëawa] as a root intimately associated with the idea of *walking along a road other than the one God wants us to use.*" [emphasis added]

"Sin is comprehensively viewed in the Old Testament as the deliberate act of

veering off the road that God wants us to travel." The best passage to illustrate this interchange is Ezekiel 18:14-31, which uses all three words.

Draw the conclusion that sin is *actively going in a direction other than the direction God commands.* The "going" pictures the succeeding events of our lives. We have no way to remain static in life; either we go on in God's way or we go in another way. Sin is moving in the wrong direction. We all

Read the command in verse 8. Ezekiel still had a free will to disobey the Lord. The temptation to abandon God's work is strong and persistent. Ezekiel would have needed to make a habit of overcoming that temptation, for he was being called to a life's workC not a temporary thrill. He spent more than twenty years preaching to Israel.

Contrast William Carey with Ezekiel as you read verses 4 through 6. Have you ever thought of foreign missions as an easier task than ministering to the people around you? It is possible for a people who have heard the truth over and over to become so hardened that they are more difficult to reach than pagans!

Ezekiel 3:7 answers the question "Why do people not listen to a preacher of God's Word?" Divide the verse into three parts according to its punctuation. The word *for* in this verse means "because." Therefore, the first sentence makes a statement, the second sentence gives a reason for the first statement, and the third sentence gives a reason for the second statement. We can reverse the order of the sentences and write *therefore* between each pair to clarify this verse: "All the house of Israel are impudent and hardhearted; *therefore* they will not hearken unto me; *therefore* they will not hearken unto you." People do not listen to God because they willfully rebel against Him; they *will not* obey. People do not listen to God's messengers because they will not listen to God.

Strong in the next verse is the same word as *stiff* in 2:4. God promises to give the prophet power to be as firm as the people are rebellious, as hardheaded as they are stubborn. An adamant is a

Hard Hearts
Review in class how the three parts of verse 7 connect logically in reverse order. Write the three parts on the board as they appear in the verse with "for" between each pair; then write them in opposite order as they appear in the student text with "therefore" between each pair.

Cookbook

From 2:9 to 3:3 Ezekiel writes that God actually had him eat a scroll. This was a symbolic act signifying that God put His own words in Ezekiel's mouth. God's message was full of sorrow (verse 10), but it tasted sweet to the prophet. That shows that it was not a literal book, because books do not taste good. (You are invited to eat part of this page if you doubt it.) You do not have to eat a spiritual book; Ezekiel did that for you and wrote it all down. His reward was becoming a Bible hero, but you get the privilege of learning God's words the easy way.

5

---

move in a certain direction in life; just by living, you move along a path. As one action follows another, the finite story of your life plays out day by day. Neutrality is impossible; you go in either God's way or the wrong way. You choose either the way of the righteous or the way of the wicked. Progress is inevitable. You cannot stop; you can only change ways! Much of the Bible draws that absolute and eternal distinction between God's people and the world's people.

Psalm 1 is an excellent illustration of this principle. It teaches that there are only two ways in life: the way of God and the way of the wicked.

For additional information note Judges 20:16, which describes slingers who could sling a stone at a hair and not *miss*. The word *miss* is actually the main word for sin, *chata'*. See also I Samuel 15:24; Job 5:24; and Isaiah 42:24, 43:27, and 53:6.

The Great Commission

Discussion

Purpose: Explain the foundational doctrines of justification and sanctification.

Follow the notes below as you explain these two doctrines. Your students must have them clearly in mind in order to understand salvation.

Ezekiel 10 through 16 records that Ezekiel was carried by the Holy Spirit to Tel-abib. The Lord apparently wanted to draw special attention to Ezekiel in order to begin preparing the prophet for his unique ministry, which was rich in object lessons.

very hard substance. Imagine the look you would get from a police officer who had seen you obviously breaking a traffic regulation. Be stubborn and argue all you want; his face will be set in stone.

In verses 10 to 17 of chapter three, the Lord commands Ezekiel to go speak to the people. Ezekiel hears the noise of the living creatures and the big wheels and then finds himself filled with righteous anger and transported to the place where many Israelites are living.

Read Ezekiel 3:17-21 before continuing. The chart below summarizes the passage.

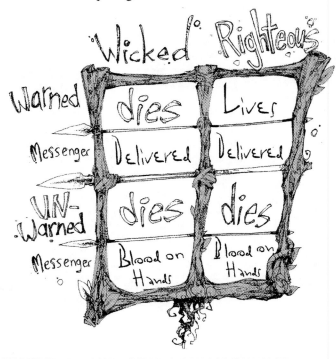

6

There are two main doctrines of salvation that we need to know to be good disciple makers. Obviously, a good soulwinner does not walk up to a lost person and start using long words to elaborate on the doctrinal elements of salvation. Because we want to be effective soulwinners, we must speak plainly and clearly as well as accurately. To speak accurately, we must be thoroughly acquainted with the biblical truths about what God does and why. The ability to explain a complex subject in simple terms is the sign that you have truly mastered the subject.

It does not take great knowledge to tell someone that Jesus died for him and wants to save him. However, our goal is to be much more than witnesses; we must be disciple makers. Making a disciple means bringing a person as far as you can toward the same level of knowledge and maturity in Christ that you yourself have reached. Furthermore, some unsaved people demand extended teaching and full explanations before they trust Christ. Every person is different—the deeper your knowledge, the more people you can effectively approach with the gospel.

Justification

The first Bible doctrine is **justification**. This term may sound like a dry bit of jargon used only by scholars, but it has everything to do with where you spend eternity. Consider this definition of

This admonition clearly implies some responsibility on the messenger's part; that is, a wicked man might have turned from sin had he been warned, and a righteous man might have avoided sin if he had been warned. We know that God chooses sinners to salvation, but this passage teaches unambiguously the parallel truth that *humans are responsible for their own obedience.*

What We Do About It: The Great Commission

We have seen that the great obstacle to evangelism and discipleship is human sin. People do not trust Christ because they do not want to; they like being sinners. So what do we do about it? The Lord Jesus outlined our task and the proper method for accomplishing it in the Great Commission.

After the Lord Jesus Christ completed His ministry on earth, He led His disciples to the top of a mountain and gave them the charge we call the Great Commission (Matt. 28:18-20). What had just happened? Only days earlier, Christ had risen alive from the dead. He who was by outward appearance a normal man had been executed as a criminal. Now He was alive again. No miracle could match that, especially when we consider that His death was not the death of an ordinary man, but that He died under the weight of God's wrath upon all human sin, suffering in an instant the justice that would have taken all mankind all of eternity to satisfy.

The risen Lord's first sentence in this passage to His disciples is "All power is given unto me in heaven and in earth." This is an incredible assertion for anyone. *Power* is properly the word *authority*, the power to rule by right. For example, the president of the United States may not be any larger or stronger than another American, but his authority is greater than any other by right of his office, giving him great "power."

Jesus had authority to give a command to the whole world. What He had commanded, was then commanding, and eventually commanded His disciples are equally His commands to us. By saying "in heaven," He shows that He is much more than an earthly king; His authority is imparted by God, from the Creator's absolute authority to do as He pleases. "On earth" shows that he is all an earthly king is but is unlimited by distance or location. He supersedes human rulers by right.

justification: "The process by which God makes a believer holy through faith and good works." A person who believes that definition does not understand his own sinfulness, how great a thing Christ did for him, nor what is truly necessary for salvation. Consequently, that person is in danger of dying unsaved.

Why is justification so serious? Read Romans 3:19-26 together in class at least twice, encouraging your students to carefully consider how each idea connects to the other concepts within the passage.

Here is a good, compact definition of justification: "To pronounce, accept, and treat as just, i.e., as, on the one hand, not penally liable, and, on the other, entitled to all the privileges due to those who have kept the law" (EDT, 593-595). Notice how the two parts of this definition of justification apply to you as a believer. First, God declares you legally not guilty of crime and therefore not liable to receive punishment. Second, God gives you the full status and position of a just person in His sight. As a justified person, you now have the right to live joyfully in His presence forever!

Sanctification

The other salvation doctrine to master is **sanctification.** By itself, sanctification can mean several things,

Ascension of Our Lord by Benjamin West

From the Bob Jones University Collection

What is the primary command in the Great Commission? Is it "Go"? "Go" is really a participle, that sets the stage for the rest of the sentence. In the verse the participle could be translated "having gone." The words *baptizing* and *teaching* are also participles. The only imperative verb is *teach*, and it is a different word than the participle *teaching* in verse 20. Its root word is the same as *disciple*, as in one of the eleven disciples standing there to hear this Great Commission (v. 16). As a verb, it means "to make someone into a disciple." The object of this verb "make disciples," is "all nations." The Lord says to make disciples of all nations. Does the English word *of* mean to make all nations into disciples? No, it means to make disciples out of all the nations. That is, some people out of every nation on earth were to be made into disciples of Christ *by* His other disciples.

Acts 8:2-4 shows that the early Christians discipled. *Make disciples* means "to bring into a master-follower relationship." We make people Christ's disciples, not our own disciples. We cause them to learn from and imitate Christ Jesus.

In apostolic days, it was truly incredible to say that one religion was meant for the whole world! Religion was very much a racial or regional characteristic. Each country had its own religion with its own gods. There was little thought of proselytizing; the Romans simply swept any new god they heard of into their pantheon (meaning "many gods") and considered him one of the divine family. The Romans did not consider any one god absolutely superior. Much less did they imagine there could be *only* one God

8

so we must clearly define what we mean. The basic meaning of *sanctify* is "to set apart" for some special purpose. To think clearly about your own sanctification, you must realize that sanctification is God's ongoing work of setting you apart from sin.

Sanctification begins at the moment of salvation. God continues the work of sanctification throughout your lifetime. As you grow in Christ, your awareness of sin steadily increases,

while your actual practice of sin steadily decreases. Because God promises to complete the "good work" (Philippians 1:6) He begins in every believer, you can trust that God will help you grow into Christian maturity. You are gradually being set apart from sin in this life. Complete sanctification will take place when you leave this life and go to live with God forever in heaven. You will be once and forever set apart from sin, completely sanctified to God.

Every ambassador for Christ must have a clear understanding of justification and sanctification in order to share the gospel most effectively. Other doctrines of salvation, such as redemption, adoption, propitiation, and glorification can be drawn together into these two concepts well enough for soulwinning and basic discipleship. Emphasize the necessary connection of doctrine to real life.

who had all power and authority and who deserved everyone's worship. Even the Jews, who should have known better, had become racially and religiously bigoted, thinking that they pleased God just by being Jews and that no one born to a different nation could ever please God as they could.

Information Service, Rome

The entrance to the Roman Pantheon, a temple dedicated to the worship of many gods

Two participles described the actions that had to accompany making disciples. Christ's disciples had to do these two things to make others into disciples. The first was *baptizing. Baptism is the one-time sign of commitment, transformation, change of direction, and new life.* It is a Christian's way of telling the world that Christ has saved him. Baptism is one commandment of Christ that every disciple must obey. This does not mean a person's salvation is dependent on baptism, for baptism is an outward sign of a spiritual reality. It is no more necessary to salvation than teaching is necessary to salvation; you do not have to learn all there is to know before you can be saved. But a true disciple will want to be baptized. He must be baptized to obey Christ perfectly.

What does baptism "in the name of" mean? The name of someone is simply a representation of that person. It is a more formal way of stating something about a person. God refers to His name as representing Himself many times in Scripture. When an ambassador acts in the name of the United States, he means he is the representative of the United States; he is acting on the country's behalf and with its authority.

9

1. Justification relates primarily to soulwinning. Justification is a one-time act of God that occurs the moment a sinner makes a genuine decision for Christ. See chapters 2-3.

2. Sanctification relates primarily to discipleship. Sanctification is an ongoing process. See chapters 4-5.

The students must understand justification in order to present the gospel accurately, even though they probably will not use that term. Remember that the gospel is true outside of man's own opinion. Even if someone misunderstands the gospel message, the truth of the gospel does not change. However, misrepresenting the gospel may hinder a person from wanting to be saved; worse, misrepresentation may lead someone into thinking he is saved when he is not!

Discussion

Point out the similarities and differences between Ezekiel's commission and the Great Commission.

Purpose: Realize that although God's message to sinners today is essentially the same as Ezekiel's message, the New Testament believer has more reason to hope for results than Ezekiel. God told Ezekiel plainly that the Israelites would not listen to him (Ezekiel 3:7). Although a few righteous people may have turned from their sin, Ezekiel spent most of his life

Baptism is a picture, a symbol of at least two spiritual realities:

1. Purification, or cleansing from sin (Acts 22:16, I Pet. 3:21). Throughout the Old and the New Testaments, washing with water represents cleansing from sin's defilement.

2. Union with Christ in His burial and resurrection (Rom. 6:3ff., Gal. 3:27).

Baptism is also an oath of loyalty to God. By being baptized in His name, we show our pledge to forever follow Him and do as He commands. Baptism has long been the best-known public symbol of a person's commitment to Christ.

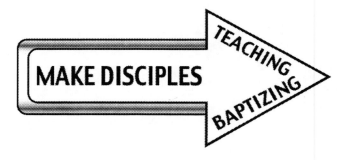

Teaching is the continual function of a disciple maker. Making another person like Christ requires *deliberate, systematic instruction in everything Christ taught.* Not only the Gospels but all the Bible is the teaching of Christ. Furthermore, we do not teach people just what the commandments are; we teach them to "observe" all those commandments. The word *observe* does not mean merely to look at, the way we use it today. It means to do a repeated action that was commanded. For example, "observing" the Sabbath means to do what God said to do on the Sabbath for every Sabbath.

Teaching people to observe Christ's commandments means that we teach them HOW to obey all those commandments and that they must obey them continually. Christ's commands are just thatC commands. They are not optional for anyone. To make a man into a disciple is to teach him what he must do in his own life to obey all the commands Christ gives.

10

prophesying to people who rejected his message.

In contrast, the Great Commisssion implies some measure of success. Though a Christian could still have a very slow and difficult ministry, the Lord indicates that the general pattern for the Church will be to evangelize and disciple converts from all nations.

Differences

Ezekiel	Christians
• Guaranteed opposition	• Assumed success
• Focus on sin	• Focus on salvation
• Local outreach	• Global outreach

Similarities

• God's sovereignty is emphasized

• Obedience is demanded

• God's personal presence is promised

Eternal Punishment

Discussion

Purpose: Understand the justice of God more fully.

Your students may have a hard time accepting that God sends people to the lake of fire forever. Show them that if we are offended at the harshness of this teaching, it is because *we do not understand the horrible nature of sin.* We like to think God is good,

Finally, the Lord calls attention (*Lo!* means "Hey!" or "Listen!") to His last promise, the pledge to accompany His disciples to the end of the age. His "I" is emphatic, so there is no question He is saying that He personally will accompany them as they go into all nations of the world. He does not mean the Holy Spirit, though the Spirit certainly does go with us; rather, He promises to be with us Himself.

Always is literally "all the days," or a promise that Christ is accompanying each of His disciples through every particular day. That stretch of days goes unto the end of *the age*, the age in which the church on earth is obeying His command to make disciples of all nations. Wherever any believer goes on any day of the entire Church Age, Christ assures that He personally is with that believer. Just as the Lord's universal absolute authority is the basis on which He gives such a command, so the promise of His perpetual presence is the assurance He will accomplish through our obedience what He intends.

What If We Don't?: Eternal Punishment

Will God really punish people who refuse to believe the gospel? Sin, at its root, is rebellion against the Lord, a willful rejection of His way. What becomes of those who will not turn from their own way, the wicked way? Is there another chance given to them in the next life? What about pagans dying in foreign lands who never heard a missionary? Did they get a different kind of chance to believe while they were on earth, or do they get a chance to believe right after death?

Does God eventually save everyone? Does the Bible exclude the possibility that God will save everyone eventually? Or does God destroy wicked people entirely, so there really is no "eternal suffering"?

What is hell like? Is it a place of oblivion, a place of regret and tortured conscience, or a physical place? Are there different levels of punishment for different people? Can you reduce your time in hell? Is hell ruled by the Devil and his demons? These are all good questions with which people have struggled for centuries. We dare not base our answers to them merely on what we think or

11

The End
"End of the world" in the A.V. means the end of this age or era of time.

The Church Age
The church age is the time span between Pentecost (fifty days after Christ's ascension) and the Rapture of the church from earth.

Heresies About Hell
Universalism is the false doctrine that teaches that God will ultimately bring everyone to heaven. Different universalists believe in different degrees of punishment for sin, but all believe that God eventually cleanses all people of sin and unites the human race in the eternal state. *Annihilationism* is the false doctrine that God obliterates the souls of wicked people so that they do not suffer consciously forever.

Both of these views are popular but unbiblical ideas of the afterlife. They are attractive because they lessen the severity of God's wrath and soothe our consciences about not witnessing to unsaved people.

Answering Objections
In class bring up some of the questions on page 11 of the student text. Ask your students if they have heard anyone ask these questions. Every question in these three paragraphs raises a common, mistaken belief about eternal punishment.

but we hate to accept that we are bad. God's goodness is beyond our moral comprehension.

Reiterate the Bible's teaching on the complete corruption of the human soul by sin. Romans 8:5-8 shows that it is impossible for an unsaved man to do *anything* truly pleasing to God. Nonetheless, the Lord Jesus bore the full penalty of human sin. When the lost go to the lake of fire, the great tragedy is not that God punishes them,

but that they refused to accept the salvation bought for them by the very blood of Christ.

Fiery Wrath
Other instances of fire picturing God's wrath are Leviticus 10:2; Numbers 26:8-10; II Kings 1:9-14; Psalm 97:3; Isaiah 29:5-6; and Malachi 4:1. It may be helpful to go over these passages to reinforce the fact that fiery wrath is not just a New Testament teaching but a continual theme in the Bible.

Halfway Hells
Catholicism does insist it is God's will for people to do more good after baptism, but baptism is the only requirement in Roman Catholicism for ultimate salvation. Movement through the Buddhist "hells" occurs through a spiritual cycle. In the earthly realm this cycle is termed *reincarnation*. Although movement through the "hells" is technically not reincarnation, the cycle is still the same.

"feel" is true; as with all other issues of eternal consequence, we must go to God's Word to learn the truth.

The Old Testament says a lot about God's wrath. We see a few references to the fact that punishment for rebelling against God is eternal, but mostly God pictures His wrath in the way He destroys His enemies on earth. For example, the way He judged Sodom and Gomorrah establishes His most prominent tool of judgment—fire (Gen. 19:24). Brimstone is sulfur, an element that burns at a lower temperature than most metals. God probably used sulfur because it is a common, cheap substance that most everyone in the ancient world was familiar with. It is not that the sulfur is not real; we have every reason to take this as literal burning sulfur falling onto the cities. It would probably have produced an effect like a huge bomb striking and destroying both cities in a massive, white-hot blast.

The Old Testament does indicate that the penalty for being God's enemy is eternal punishment. The prophet Isaiah warned people of God's terrible wrath in chapter 33, verse 14, when he said, "The sinners in Zion [Jerusalem] are afraid; fearfulness hath surprised the hypocrites. Who among us shall dwell with the devouring fire? who among us shall dwell with everlasting burnings?"

Isaiah's strongest passage on eternal punishment is located at the very end of his sixty-six-chapter book. Read Isaiah 66:15-24. This passage is set in the future, when the Lord will rule the new heaven and new earth directly. Verse 17 describes sins related to idolatry, while verse 19 shows that the whole world will acknowledge the Lord as God.

Halfway Hells

The Roman Catholic Church teaches that most people who were baptized go to purgatory after death. Purgatory is a place of limited suffering; a soul stays there until it is purged of all the sin the person committed but did not experience forgiveness for while he was alive. Buddhism teaches there are fourteen different hells, seven hot and seven cold, through which a person may move if he is too bad during his earthly incarnations. Neither of these views is supported by Scripture.

The final verse grips us by claiming that those who worship God forever will be able to see the bodies of people who never repented of sin. The description of unquenchable fire and an undying worm very likely was an allusion to the massive garbage disposal area in the valley of Ben-Hinnom, where Israelites burned their garbage with a continuous fire. The steady supply of garbage kept the fires from ever completely dying out. What the fire did not destroy, worms ate. Imagine how much the worms would have to eat in a place where flowed an endless stream of rotten food, the carcasses of dead animals, and other assorted wastes! Thus, the valley of Ben-Hinnom was a very visible picture of the eternal destiny of people who died in rebellion against God.

Photo by Bryan Smith

The Valley of Ben-Hinnom (Gehenna)

Modern Gehenna
This shot looks south from the southern edge of modern Jerusalem. In ancient times, neither the buildings nor the landscaping would have been there.

Some people find a measure of comfort about the afterlife by believing that sinners sent to hell are destroyed there. Yes, they say, hell may be a horrible place, but souls sent there will eventually cease to exist; their suffering will come to an end. But the New Testament makes it undeniable that hell is a place of endless suffering. The Lord Jesus Himself, who said so much about the love and mercy of God, who died in the place of sinners and rose again so that they might avoid hell and live forever with God, preached on the horrors of hell many times. In Mark 9:47-48 the Lord quoted Isaiah 66:24. Christ taught in Matthew 18:8 and 25:41-46 that hell lasts forever. He says in Matthew 13:42 that people in hell suffer consciously.

13

Since the rich man asks that Lazarus be sent to his brothers on earth (vv. 27-28), and since the Lord tells this story as a matter of history, it is apparent that the wicked dead go to a temporary place of suffering different from the lake of fire. There, they await the final judgment of Revelation 20.

Luke 16 contains the Lord's most vivid warning of hell. In the story of the rich man and Lazarus, the rich man, in hell, asks that Lazarus, in heaven, might wet his finger and touch the rich man's tongue, for, he says, "I am tormented in this flame." That tiny bit of relief is all the former master of much asks. He is awake, alert to suffering, and has his memory intact.

The Book of Revelation gives us a preview of what will happen at the end of the Church Age. First, chapter 20 describes the binding of Satan during a one-thousand-year period and the first resurrection. Read verses 2 through 6 of Revelation 20.

Verse 7 starts the description of the last phase in the long rebellion against God. Satan is released for his "little season" (v. 3) to deceive the nations of the world one more time and lead them to besiege Jerusalem, the city that has been the Lord's earthly headquarters during that thousand-year period. Although the account may make us expect a dramatic final battle, Scripture dispenses with this last, largest uprising in a single sentence at the end of verse 9. This verse gives the final picture of God's wrath. It is consistent with the other judgments by fire. Now there remains the grim reality pictured in all preceding judgments.

First, the Devil is thrown into the lake that burns with fire and brimstone. The Beast and the False Prophet, two human beings who have given themselves entirely to Satan's service, are already in the lake of fire, having been thrown there at the beginning of the thousand years (see Rev. 19:20, which says plainly they were thrown in alive). The two chief rebels have not been annihilated by the lake; they are still in it when Satan joins them. The final phrase in 20:10 cannot be more clear that suffering in the lake is unending and eternal.

Verses 11 to 15 then record the last judgment, the second resurrection. This includes all people who ever lived who were not saved by faith in Jesus Christ. With heaven and earth gone, there is nothing in the universe on which to focus attention except the great white throne on which the Judge sits. We know from John 5:21-23 and II Timothy 4:1 that He is the Lord Jesus Christ. He who died to save all men has the right and authority to condemn forever those who rebelled against Him and rejected His offer of salvation.

The Book of Life is opened. A book of life was a birth registry recording the names of all babies born in a city. This is God's Book of Life recording the name of every person born into His family. Other books, containing records of every person's life, are opened. People who do not accept the salvation Christ provides must be judged by their works, and these books tell of the evil they have done.

Have you ever met someone who considered himself good enough to get into heaven? Do you know people who imagine all their pluses and minuses weighed in a giant scale to see if their pluses will tip the balance and get them into heaven? These people will receive exactly the kind of evaluation they expect. However, they must measure up to God's standard of righteousness to merit heaven. This passage and many others show that no human being who has ever lived is good enough to earn God's favor and merit life in heaven. People who stand before God with only their own works will all see their minuses heavily outweigh their pluses, for they will learn that Isaiah 64:6 is true in saying that "all our righteousnesses are as filthy rags" to our holy God.

History of the Book of Life
According to the *Zondervan Pictorial Encyclopedia of the Bible*, the New Testament usage of "the Book of Life" is based on Old Testament references to God's book. This book contained the names of the righteous (Exodus 32:32 and Psalm 69:28). The concept of writing down the names of the righteous probably stemmed from the practice of writing out genealogies (Nehemiah 7:5ff; Psalm 87:6; and Jeremiah 22:30).

Superficial Goodness
Romans 8:5-8 says that it is impossible for an unsaved man to do anything truly pleasing to God. Even when an unsaved man does an apparently good thing, it is worthless in God's sight because man's every act is motivated by pride. Because of man's sinful nature, his actions are destined to lead to evil. There really are no "pluses" for an unsaved man to put in the balance scale at the judgment. Steer your students away from the idea that lost people do good things in God's sight; to God's unclouded and unbiased vision, we are all hopelessly sinful.

Reaching the Lost
The last paragraph may describe one of your students. You may want to take time to ask your class members if they are expecting their merits to get them into heaven. Remind them verbally that no amount of good works will get a person into God's presence in heaven.

Analysis of Questions

2. At the Great White Throne Judgment, everyone who died unsaved will be judged by his works and found lacking.

5. Luke 16 is apparently not referring to the lake of fire because life on earth is still normal. The lake of fire comes after the Millennium.

6. Answer *b* is true but is not what the text calls the greatest reason.

True or False

__T__ 1. In Ezekiel 2, the word *stiff* carries the idea of physical strength.

__F__ 2. No one is ever judged according to his works.

Short/Long Answer

3. Why did God have Ezekiel eat a scroll?

   Eating it signified that God put His own words in Ezekiel's mouth.

4. What is the primary command in the Great Commission?

   "teach" or "make disciples"

5. What verse discussed in the text makes it clearest that those thrown into the lake of fire suffer consciously forever?

   Revelation 19:20 or 20:10

Multiple Choice

__D__ 6. What is the greatest reason that evangelism is difficult?

   A. It costs too much.
   B. It is not natural.
   C. Sinners cannot understand the gospel.
   D. Sinners do not think that they are sinners.

_D_ 7. What is sin?

    A. A willful refusal to obey God's authority
    B. Going out of bounds and doing what God forbids
    C. Lots of repeated mistakes
    D. A and B

_A_ 8. Which of these best explains Jesus' authority in Matthew 28:18?

    A. His right to tell everyone what to do
    B. His ability to do whatever He wants
    C. His position as the greatest earthly king
    D. None of these

_B_ 9. Which of the following is clearly true of someone who claims to believe in Christ but refuses water baptism?

    A. He has not believed in the name of Christ.
    B. He is not fully obedient to Scripture.
    C. He is not really saved.
    D. He draws attention to the spiritual reality of baptism.

_A_ 10. Which of the following is a true statement about water baptism?

    A. Water baptism is a Christian's public declaration that he belongs to God.
    B. Water baptism unites a believer to Christ.
    C. Water baptism removes sin.
    D. All of the above

7. Answer *c* is a result of sin.

8. Answer *c* is true but is incorporated into answer *a*, which applies to all people.

9. Answers *a* and *c* are equivalent to each other, though possibly true of someone refusing baptism. Answer *b* is the only answer that is universally true of all people who refuse to be baptized.

10. Answers *b* and *c* refer to the results of spiritual baptism, not water baptism. Spiritual baptism occurs the moment someone believes in Christ.

CHAPTER TWO

Thinking Biblically About Witnessing
②
Memory Verses: John 15:16 and Acts 1:8

Goals

Students should
1. Build a desire to witness regularly to unsaved people.
2. Accept the Bible's instructions for witnessing.

Objectives

Students should be able to
1. Discuss the Lord's principles of personal evangelism.
2. List five reasons witnessing is highly important.
3. Describe the four different responses to the gospel seen in the parable of the sower (or soils).

In this chapter and the next, we begin to study the first part of disciple making, personal evangelism. In Chapter 1 we laid the scriptural foundation for disciple making by examining what sin is like, what Christ said we should do for sinners, and what happens to sinners who never repent. With the biblical reasons for making disciples in mind, we want to discuss the skills and practical methods useful to that end.

Romans 10:13-14 teaches clearly that someone must hear the gospel in order to be saved. Though God saves people, He sends other people to *evangelize* them. To evangelize means "to proclaim the good message." God chooses to use imperfect men to proclaim the gospel because this method gives Him the opportunity to show His power in the midst of human weakness. Personal evangelism is telling someone that Christ died for his sins and wants him to repent of sin and be saved. Christians must tell others about Jesus Christ.

Part of this course requires you to practice personal evangelism. The particulars of personal evangelism change with circumstances. Witnessing to others about Christ is basically simple, but it is still a skill that improves with practice. You have to follow the scriptural principles in whatever way is most appropriate to your situation.

Chapters 2 and 3 are adapted from *Witnessing for Christ* by Stephen Hankins. Chapter 2 provides the proper scriptural mindset for personal evangelism and Chapter 3 outlines an excellent model to follow in an average witnessing encounter. As you read, imagine how the principles described will translate into real life as you go out to witness for Christ.

Overview

Having laid the foundational beliefs in the first chapter, we now begin learning how to make someone into a disciple for Christ. Disciple making is a two-step process. The first step is personal evangelism—leading an unsaved person to trust Christ. The second step is personal discipleship—teaching a new Christian to think and act more and more like Jesus Christ.

Chapters 2 and 3 deal with the first step in disciple making, personal evangelism. Adopted from *Witnessing for Christ* by Stephen Hankins, the student text first establishes the biblical mindset for witnessing and then offers a practical plan for witnessing.

19

Exercise: Christ the Soulwinner

Goal: Learn from two examples of Christ's personal evangelism how to reach people from any social or religious background and lead them to trust Christ for salvation.

The Lord Jesus Christ came into the world primarily to save sinners (I Timothy 1:15). He is an expert at leading people to trust Him for salvation, whether he wins them through preaching or personal evangelism. The following discussions of John 3:1-21 and John 4:1-30 provide a detailed look at two instances of personal evangelism from the Lord's earthly ministry. As you take your students through these discussions, point out how the Lord steers the conversation toward salvation. He gives Nicodemus and the Samaritan woman the necessary truths of the gospel, challenges their misconceptions, and brings them to a point of decision. His approach provides an excellent lesson in what to say to a lost person and how to say it.

These two cases also show His ministry to individuals at either end of the social and religious spectrums. Christ gave each the same message, but He approached each in ways suited to the lost person's own personality and situation. (Highlight the differences between Nicodemus and the Samaritan woman by following the instructions in the marginal note on page 20.)

Nicodemus Versus The Samaritan Woman

Read John 3:1-21 in class. You might have each of seven students read three verses out loud. Elicit from your class some observations about Nicodemus, writing characteristics in a vertical list on the board or overhead. Encourage the students to think about Nicodemus's background, education, motives for coming to Jesus, and future plans. Fill in information from the list of characteristics below if needed. Do not allow unfounded conjecture about Nicodemus.

Read John 4:1-30 in class. Students may again read the passage aloud, three verses at a time. Follow the same procedure as above to collect a list of characteristics of the Samaritan woman. Write these characteristics in a separate vertical list on the board or overhead. When finished, compare and contrast the two lists to highlight the differences in the people to whom the Lord witnessed, the different approaches He used, and the different results He encountered.

Nicodemus's Characteristics

1. A man
2. A Jew
3. Highly religious
4. Politically prominent
5. Wealthy
6. Came to Jesus
7. Makes no overt profession but appears converted later

Samaritan Woman's Characteristics

1. A woman
2. A Samaritan
3. Irreligious
4. Politically insignificant
5. Poor
6. Jesus came to her
7. Publicly professes salvation and shows immediate fruit

Introduction

Paul says, "For the preaching of the cross is to them that perish foolishness; but unto us which are saved it is the power of God" (I Cor. 1:18). There are two basic responses to the gospel of Christ. Some reject it because they view it as nonsense, and others accept it as the power of God to transform their lives. Christians, those who have been changed by the message of the cross, are obligated to present that message to others; they are representatives of Christ to a hostile world. Paul writes, "Now then we are ambassadors for Christ, as though God did beseech you by us: we pray you in Christ's stead, be ye reconciled to God" (II Cor. 5:20). Witnessing for Christ is not the responsibility of pastors and evangelists alone. Every believer is responsible to proclaim the good news of Christ. Note that in II Corinthians Paul addresses all Christians, not simply preachers.

The believer may be tempted to shun his responsibility to witness because of a fear of speaking or a fear of being rejected by others. But the believer must always remember that "God hath not given us the spirit of fear; but of power, and of love, and of a sound mind" (II Tim. 1:7). The believer must rest in the assurance of Acts 1:8, which states, "But ye shall receive power, after that the Holy Ghost is come upon you: and ye shall be witnesses unto me both in Jerusalem, and in all Judea, and in Samaria, and unto the uttermost part of the earth." The Lord will empower the believer to overcome the fear of speaking to others about Christ.

Accepting the reproach of the gospel is an essential part of being a faithful believer. Jesus says, "For whoever shall be ashamed of me and of my words, of him shall the Son of man be ashamed, when he shall come in his own glory, and in his Father's, and of the holy angels" (Luke 9:26). Believers cannot and should not try to avoid the reproach of Christ. Peter reminds us, "If ye be reproached for the name of Christ, happy are ye; for the spirit of glory and of God resteth upon you: on their part he is evil spoken of, but on your part he is glorified" (I Pet. 4:14).

20

Use the diagrams in the back of the book to show your class the flow of the conversations. It is much easier to understand how each sentence relates to the others when you see the conversations charted in columns with the key words highlighted.

Discussion: John 3:1-21—The Religious Man

1: Nicodemus was a respected religious leader, a highly educated scholar, and a prominent figure in politics. He embodies high society. He appears to have been a basically good man, not an odorous hypocrite or a corrupt bureaucrat.

Application: No one is too high for the gospel. Do not neglect witnessing to the wealthy or to religious leaders, such as Roman Catholic priests and Jewish rabbis.

2: Most Jewish leaders despised the Lord. To avoid attracting their attention, Nicodemus came to Jesus at night. Nicodemus knew the Scriptures well and probably suspected that Jesus of Nazareth was indeed the Messiah. His first sentence was quite complimentary, coming from the chief rabbi to a carpenter!

However, had Nicodemus understood the Scripture well enough to know that Jesus was the Messiah, he would have realized how disrespectful he and the other Jewish leaders actually were. Christ did not even acknowledge the

I. The Importance of Witnessing

When something valuable is lost, men go to great lengths to find it. Mel Fisher, one of the greatest treasure hunters of the twentieth century, illustrates this truth. In 1969 Fisher formed Treasure Salvors, Inc., with family members, hired divers, and other assistants. They then began to search for the *Nuestra Señora de Atocha,* a Spanish galleon which sank near Key West during a hurricane in 1622. Reportedly, the galleon was carrying over 600 pounds of gold, 1,038 silver bars, and 250,000 silver coins; the value of the treasure was estimated at four hundred million dollars.

In 1973 Fisher's son Dirk found the ship's anchor and three silver bars in shallow water about seven miles from the ship's actual resting place. Because of its location, Dirk's find proved to be misleading for the search party; the "false find" cost Fisher several years. More importantly, it was also tragic: Dirk continued to search in the same treacherous waters, and two years later his boat capsized, killing him and his wife.

The search for the *Atocha* cost Fisher a great deal of money, many years, and even his son's life. However, his efforts were finally rewarded on July 20, 1985. During a routine search, divers found the *Atocha.* Kane, Mel Fisher's younger son, jubilantly radioed the news to his father in Key West. The *Atocha* has since proved to be the most lucrative oceanic find to date. Although this story deals with monetary treasures, the believer should find an important lesson in this account. We should make a diligent effort to seek the lost who are in bondage to sin; they are of inestimable value to God.

A. W. Tozer, a pastor and well-known author who is now with the Lord, once wrote, "Men are lost but not abandoned: that is

---

Sinful to the Core
Ask students what they think the answer is to this question: Can an unsaved person do something that pleases God? Have all those who answer "yes" raise their hands; then ask all those who answer "no" to raise their hands. Collect some explanations and defenses for the students' answers.

Now have one student read Isaiah 64:6 and another read Proverbs 15:8. Point out that, although unsaved people can do things that seem good and right, God's only message to the lost is a call to repent and be saved. Apart from Christ, even a good deed is never right in God's eyes. Man is thoroughly corrupt. Whether we like it or not, the answer to the above question is "No, sinners cannot please God."

Biblical Balance
Focus on the wickedness and helplessness of man in order to balance the text's focus on personal responsibility. Providing this balance does not contradict the student text. We are helplessly sinful and responsible to choose right at the same time. You might explain this paradox by saying that, although the ability to do anything pleasing to God comes from Him in the first place, we still have to take advantage of that ability by choosing to do right.

---

intended compliment but immediately steered the great rabbi toward his own need of a personal Savior.

Application: Do not be deflected by flattery. A surprisingly potent weapon, flattery is employed by people who like to be friends with everyone. They want you to like them and be nice to them, but they do not want to think about heavy matters like sin, guilt, and the crucifixion of Christ.

3-4: Jews in the first century thought

they deserved eternal life just because they were Jews. They also thought they could earn favor with God by righteous works. Nicodemus had misunderstood the Old Testament so badly that he was completely taken aback at Christ's statement that a man must be "born again."

5-7: A regenerated man understands that a person must experience the second birth wrought by the Holy Spirit. Unfortunately, Nicodemus was not

such a man. The word for "born" is the word for a father's begetting children. We use the transitive verb "fathered [a child]" to give the same meaning. Nicodemus heard that he had to be "fathered" by the Spirit to enter the kingdom of God! Christ directly confronted him with the need for spiritual rebirth apart from lawkeeping.

Application: There is no substitute for getting to the point. You can use the same image of spiritual birth to get

what the Scriptures teach and that is what the church is commissioned to declare." Every Christian is commissioned to carry the gospel of Christ to the unsaved. To meet this responsibility, undaunted by obstacles and abounding with hope, the believer must think biblically about the task. The following are several teachings in the New Testament that emphasize the supreme importance of evangelizing the lost.

Christ came to seek and to save the lost. Jesus clearly revealed the nature of His ministry. He said, "The Son of man is come to save that which was lost" (Matt. 18:11). The Scriptures teach that Christ healed many who were sick, taught His disciples, and by His life and death provided an example for us to follow (cf. I Pet. 2:21). Although every aspect of Christ's earthly ministry was vital, of extreme importance were His redemptive proclamations and work. Even New Testament teaching concerning the incarnation emphasizes Christ's redemptive mission. Paul writes, "But when the fulness of the time was come, God sent forth his Son, made of a woman, made under the law, to redeem them that were under the law, that we might receive the adoption of sons" (Gal. 4:4-5).

Christ's desire to see men rescued from their lost condition is demonstrated by both His mass evangelistic efforts and His many personal evangelistic encounters. (Mark 2:13-17; Luke 19:1-10, 23:32-43; John 1:35-42; and John 4:1-30 are a few examples of Christ's efforts in personal evangelism.) Of course, His message of deliverance from sin was made possible by His death on the cross. The time, effort, and sacrifice that Christ devoted to His evangelistic ministry should compel every Christian to make witnessing a top priority in his life.

Christ commanded His disciples to reach the lost. Christ's design for the ministry of the disciples is most clearly seen in the Great Commission (Matt. 28:18-20; Mark 16:15; Luke 24:46-49). These passages outline several vital truths that underscore the importance of witnessing. First, the Lord Jesus promises His presence and authority to those who witness. Second, believers must spread the gospel throughout the world. Third, the proclamation of the gospel will result in men's identifying with Christ by baptism and becoming known as part of the body of Christ. Finally,

The Great Redeemer
In Galatians 4:4-5 "the fulness of the time" simply refers to the time when everything had been fully prepared by God for Christ's coming. Those "under the law" are all believers, Old and New Testament. We are all condemned by God's holy law but redeemed by Christ, who not only took upon Himself the penalty of the law but also fully kept the law.

Harmonizing the Commissions
Have students read Matthew 28:18-20 and Luke 24:46-49. Compare these commissions in class, pointing out differences and similarities. Ask the class members what they think Christ really said. The answer of course is that He said everything recorded in any gospel; each evangelist wrote what was appropriate to his own purpose. We do not have a verbatim transcription of the entire Great Commission, and we do not need one. The Holy Spirit has preserved exactly as much as is relevant to us.

almost anyone's attention. It can be more vivid and less familiar than "saved." Simply quoting these verses is a way to arrest a man's attention.

8: This verse illustrates the nature of spiritual reality. "Spirit" and "wind" are the same word in the New Testament language; thus, they form a deliberate play on words. When the wind blows, you cannot see it or predict what it will do next, but you certainly do not deny that it is real!

Likewise, when the Spirit acts, you cannot deny His reality, but neither can you see Him nor predict where He will act next.

Application: A natural illustration makes another effective means of stimulating a person's interest. You can copy the Lord's illustration from this verse, or you may make up another of your own.

9: Nicodemus's question showed his bewilderment when confronted with

spiritual truth. Even with all his knowledge, Nicodemus had failed to understand that birth into God's kingdom is by a supernatural act of God, not by any human effort or man-made system of religion.

10: The Lord responded with a question that actually reads, "Are you *the teacher* of Israel, and don't know these things?" However shocking Jesus' words may have sounded to Nicodemus, Christ was setting forth instruction about conversion must precede all other teachings concerning Christlikeness. *wed*

Christ sent the Holy Spirit to empower believers to reach the lost. In its scope, Acts 1:8 is similar to the Great Commission. Here Christ commands believers to witness in Jerusalem, Judea, Samaria, and the whole world. In other words, Christians today should witness everywhere and at all times. In order to help the Christian meet this responsibility, the Holy Spirit indwells the believer. The Spirit of God leads the Christian (Rom. 8:14) and strengthens him (Eph. 3:16) for the task of proclaiming the truth with boldness.

Christ expects us to witness as part of our worship of Him. How better can the Christian honor Christ and show his confidence in the Lord's power to save than by witnessing to others? Certainly the apostle Paul understood this principle and viewed his efforts in winning the lost as an offering that he presented to the Lord. He says, "That I should be the minister of Jesus Christ to the Gentiles, ministering the gospel of God, that the offering up of the Gentiles might be acceptable, being sanctified by the Holy Ghost" (Rom. 15:16).

Christ views witnessing as evidence of the genuineness of our salvation. Jesus says, "Whosoever therefore shall confess me before men, him will I confess also before my Father which is in heaven. But whosoever shall deny me before men, him will I also deny before my Father which is in heaven" (Matt. 10:32-33). Romans 10:10-11 reiterates this teaching: "For with the heart man believeth unto righteousness; and with the mouth confession is made unto salvation. For the scripture saith, Whosoever believeth on him shall not be ashamed." If a person is truly saved, he will testify of Christ's saving power that he has personally experienced.

An Acceptable Offering
"The offering up of the Gentiles" refers to Paul's work of evangelizing many non-Jewish people groups. The image of an offering is used frequently for any work (including prayer) done in God's service.

Why Witnessing Is Important

1. Christ came to seek and to save the lost.
2. Christ commanded His disciples to reach the lost.
3. Christ sent the Holy Spirit to empower believers to reach the lost.
4. Christ expects us to witness as part of our worship to Him.
5. Christ views witnessing as evidence of the genuineness of our salvation.

23

---

the teachings that had been revealed in the Old Testament.

Next the Lord established the authority and reliability of what He was teaching (11-13). Then he gave an illustration to picture His upcoming crucifixion (14-15), the central purpose of His life on earth and the work that made it possible for Nicodemus to be born again.

The narrating voice of John picks up somewhere between verses 10 and 22,

most likely at the "for" in verse 16. He elaborates on the mission of Christ and the way of salvation. Though the words are no longer quotations, they probably summarize what Jesus told Nicodemus that night. The two men sat in the dark night, one listening in rapt attention as the other expounded the most remarkable truths ever spoken on earth.

18: These last verses offer an important commentary on the nature of sin.

John writes a warning to everyone who will not believe. Refusing to believe in Christ is a sin worthy of "condemnation," meaning no less than eternal punishment in the lake of fire.

19-20: Man's problem and the reason for it are exposed. Men are not only bound in darkness; they *like* darkness—even love it! Man's affection for evil shows that sin is a matter of corruption at the deepest level of the heart. Human beings by nature resist

II. Various Responses to Witnessing (Matt. 13)

Our Lord taught that not everyone who hears the gospel will respond with saving faith. The parable of the sower (or more appropriately, the parable of the soils) teaches this truth. Christ related the parable in Matthew 13:3-9 and explained it in verses 18-23. The reader must not conclude from the three types of poor soil that seventy-five percent of the people to whom he witnesses will not respond favorably. Christ did not intend the parable to reflect the actual percentage of positive and negative responses. Rather, Christ emphasized that the believer can expect varying responses to his evangelistic efforts. In reality, even the positive and negative responses will vary.

Scripture parallel: Acts 17:30-32a

The Hard-Hearted Hearer (v. 19) The hard soil in verse 19 is described as "the way side." This word refers to a well-worn path beside a plowed field. Some of the seed that the sower scatters falls on the path but does not penetrate the hard ground. When confronted with the Word, some people, like hardened paths, do not let the message penetrate their hearts. Someone may not receive the gospel because he does not understand the message  (v. 19). This tragedy should not be the result of an unclear presentation; rather, it should happen only because the hearer refuses to understand or accept the truth.

Scripture parallel: John 6:60-66

The Impulsive Hearer (vv. 20-21) Verses 20 and 21 mention the emotional or impulsive response. This type of ground is described as "stony"; in other words, there is a thick slab of limestone inches below the surface which does not permit roots to go deep enough to obtain water and nutrients. Therefore, when the sun

24

God. The reason given is that Christ ("the light") exposes their evil deeds. Coming into contact with Jesus Christ shows a man that everything he does is evil. Men do not like learning this lesson. We tend to satisfy ourselves with the notion that we are basically good and that our works are good.

Application: Do not be surprised or discouraged when people reject the gospel. You may have made mistakes in your presentation, but people reject

God because they hate Him, not because you are a poor witness. Most people become defensive when confronted with their sins. You can only bring people to the point of decision. If they refuse Christ, you can do no more.

We are not told that Nicodemus trusted Christ as his Savior that night. He must have had a very hard time accepting that he had missed the whole point of the Scripture he had spent his life studying and teaching. He also knew

that he would have to face enormous peer pressure if he followed Christ. Allegiance to Christ probably would have cost him his rank and position. Nevertheless, John 7:50-51 shows Nicodemus trying to defend Jesus from the rest of the Sanhedrin, and John 19:39 records that Nicodemus had the courage to take the body of Jesus Christ off the cross and bury Him while all of the disciples hid. Remember that at least two years separated the first and the last appearances of

is hot, the warm soil incubates the seed and causes quick growth but eventually scorches the plant because the roots cannot get water. The heat of the sun is analogous to persecution, and the quick growth to a thoughtless, emotional, or impulsive response. If a person does not consider the cost before trusting Christ, he will not stand firm when hard times come. Obviously, this description refers to a person who has made a hasty, emotional decision but who does not demonstrate true, saving faith in Christ.

Proper Preaching
Christ always preached the gospel properly, but he received various responses. The negative responses show that even when a preacher does everything right, people can still reject the gospel.

Scripture parallel: II Timothy 4:10

The Unproductive Hearer (v. 22) Of all the responses to the seed of the Word, the one represented by thorny ground is the most difficult to explain. This soil receives the seed, and there appears to be some life; yet sinful influences keep the plant from bearing any fruit. The meaning becomes clear, however, when one recognizes that Jesus is speaking of *observable* responses to the gospel. It is impossible to determine the spiritual condition of this type of person, but this ambiguity is precisely the point of Christ's teaching. Some seem to profess Christ genuinely, but they bear no fruit. It is difficult to tell whether they are carnal Christians (I Cor. 3:1-2) or lost men (Matt. 7:15-20). Scripture teaches that at times there is simply no way to know the true heart condition of people (Matt. 13:24-30).

The Genuine Hearer (v. 23) The last kind of soil is "good ground." Sowing upon this type of ground results in growth and fruit. The quantity of fruit may vary, but the harvest is abundant. This soil describes the person who receives the incorruptible seed of the Word and is born again (I Pet. 1:23). He receives the Word, obeys it, and begins to bear fruit.

Scripture parallel: II Timothy 1:3-7

25

Nicodemus. Slowly and with timid steps, Nicodemus eventually turned from the world and followed Christ.

Discussion: John 4:1-30—The Woman at the Well, Samaritan and Sinner

1-3: After leaving Nicodemus, Jesus went with His disciples into the countryside of Judea, baptizing repentant Jews. The Pharisees were a large religious party who were the dominant Jewish political power. When they heard that Jesus' disciples had baptized more people than even John the Baptist, whom they already hated and feared, they began taking steps to arrest or assassinate the Lord. Of course, a conflict was inevitable. However, since the Son still had much work to do before going to the cross, the Father made sure that Jesus' enemies did not crucify Christ at this early stage of the Messiah's earthly ministry.

4: John writes that the Lord *had* to go through Samaria, as if He insisted on an unusual or unnecessary course of action. We know from accounts in the New Testament that Jews and Samaritans were bitter antagonists. Jews ordinarily traveled around Samaria to go from Judea to Galilee, although it was a slightly longer journey.

5: Verse 5 connects the setting to its Old Testament background. The Old Testament does not record Jacob's

III. *T*he Right Attitude for Witnessing (Luke 15)

The longest New Testament passage that concerns reaching the lost is Luke 15. This thirty-two-verse chapter contains Christ's most concentrated instruction on the subject. Here Jesus responds to the objection of outwardly pious religionists to His efforts to reach the lost, and He gives positive instruction to believers concerning how to approach the lost.

The passage contains three parables about lost items: the lost sheep (vv. 4-7), the lost coin (vv. 8-10), and the lost son, commonly called the prodigal son (vv. 11-32). In each parable, the lost item represents a person who is lost in sin. In each case, the lost item or person is found. These parables emphasize two necessary characteristics for reaching the lost.

Be aggressive. Three vital qualities characterize this aggressiveness in reaching the lost. First, *persistence* marks aggressive witnessing. The shepherd sought until he found the lost sheep (v. 4). The woman searched her house, sweeping every corner, until she found her missing coin (v. 8). Although the father never left his estate to search for his son, the passage implies that he eagerly anticipated his son's return ("when he was yet a great way off, his father saw him"—v. 20).

Preoccupation with the lost is a second characteristic of aggressive witnessing. Although the shepherd had ninety-nine remaining sheep, he was intensely concerned about the lost one (v. 4). The woman still possessed nine coins, but she naturally wanted to find the one she had lost (v. 8). The father had one remaining son and a great estate, but he never lost his intense desire for his lost son to return (v. 20).

Third, this aggressiveness is tempered by *compassion*. When the shepherd found the sheep, he carried it on his shoulders back to the fold (v. 5). When the father saw his son from a great distance, he had compassion on him (v. 20).

Aggressiveness is necessary for the effective soulwinner, for the lost generally do not seek the Lord. They are usually satisfied with their way of life and usually do not worry about their fate. The believer is responsible to seek these lost people, warn them of

Reaching the Lost Righteously

The Lord gives these parables in answer to the Pharisees who criticized Him for spending so much time with obviously worldly people. (The Pharisees called the worldly people "sinners.") The Lord spent time with lost people (the kind who were obviously lost) without engaging in their sin or picking up their bad habits. Likewise, we can spend time in personal contact with worldly people, even in an informal setting (Christ ate meals at their houses), and still maintain our distinctive feature, our holiness. Christ is our example to follow in this righteous approach to reaching the lost, as in all things. However, it is imperative to remember that a Christian must be mature in order to influence others for good without being influenced for evil. A teenager may have a good ministry to his unsaved friends if he maintains a strong and consistent Christian testimony, but an immature Christian teen may be led down a wrong path by associating too much with worldly teens. Carefully consider the spiritual maturity of your students and exhort them accordingly.

---

giving of Sychar (Samaria) to Joseph, but when the descendants of Joseph (subdivided into the tribes of Ephraim and Manasseh) entered Canaan, this area was part of their allotment.

When the Assyrians conquered the Northern Kingdom of Israel in 722 B.C., they deported many of the wealthy and educated Israelites. The Assyrians brought into Samaria other ethnic groups to replace the deported Jews and to dilute Israel's national

identity. This method of cutting back Jewish influence defused the threat of the Israelites revolting against their conquerors. The remaining Hebrews intermarried with these pagans and mixed the worship of false deities with the worship of God, producing the Samaritan race and religion.

6: Notice that the Lord deliberately placed himself among people of spiritual need. He took His rest at a place where He was likely to encounter a na-

tive. On the other hand, He was not in fresh physical condition. His request for water is not invented—He really was thirsty. He put Himself in position to witness even though He did not "feel like it" in the human sense.

7: Women normally drew water in the morning because the temperature was cool and they could use the water all day. This lone Samaritan woman came at the sixth hour (see verse 6), which was probably noon. Apparently she did

the consequences of their sin, and lead them to Christ, the true Shepherd.

Be optimistic. Not everyone who hears the gospel will accept the Lord, but many will. Although the parable of the sower emphasizes the variety of responses, Christ's three parables of the lost things do not share this emphasis. These parables highlight the *finding* of the lost item, as well as the consequent rejoicing. The fact that every lost item is found is a cause for optimism.

In addition, the parables consistently note the *rejoicing* that takes place after the lost item or person is found. The repentant sinner brings joy to the heart of God (v. 7). When the ungodly turn to the Lord, the angels rejoice (v. 10). The household of faith engages in joyful celebration when a lost one comes to Christ (vv. 22-24, 32). These responses should encourage the believer in his evangelistic efforts.

Another encouraging aspect of these parables is that the believer's responsibility in evangelism is *reasonable*. Jesus twice stated that the heavens rejoice over even one sinner who repents (vv. 7, 10). God does not set unreasonable or impossible goals for the believer. A Christian should not be discouraged by the sheer number of lost people; by God's grace he should seek to win one person at a time.

Righteous Rejoicing
Point out to your class that, though rejoicing when someone says he has just been saved is the right thing to do, it can encourage some people to seek attention or popularity by claiming to have gotten saved when they really have not. Your students must be balanced when reacting to someone who announces that he just trusted Christ. They should show their joy but not elevate the person to the point that someone else would profess salvation just to receive attention.

27

not want the company of other women or was shunned by them due to her sinful reputation.

The Lord's request violated two customs: first, unrelated men and women did not commonly speak in public, and second, Jews and Samaritans did not commonly speak to each other at all. Jesus did not allow an unnecessary cultural norm or a racial barrier to prevent His personal evangelism.

9: Both surprises are clear from the woman's response in verse 9. We do not know what emotion colored this woman's response, but her words were probably not at all cordial. The Lord put Himself at a disadvantage to her, giving her a chance to do Him a favor. He was not afraid to be vulnerable before the person He witnessed to.

10: Just as He had with Nicodemus, Jesus avoided letting the woman get Him on a tangent. He was not defensive or argumentative. His statement in verse 10 was couched in a leading manner that took the conversation smoothly up to a spiritual level and invited the woman's curiosity.

"Living water" was a regular phrase for running water, as in a stream or brook, as opposed to still water in a pond or lake. Running water was preferable to still water because it was cleaner and easier to access. Jesus used the phrase in a figurative sense, though He knew the woman would not

IV. God's Part in Witnessing

Personal evangelism is a divine/human endeavor. Only God can deliver a man from the consequences of sin, yet God has decided to use His servants to reach lost men. However, the believer's evangelistic efforts will not be successful if he does not rely upon the power of God. Salvation is a supernatural event in the life of a sinful man; no amount of human effort alone can save a lost man.

God answers prayer. Obedient Christians see their prayers answered (John 15:7). If a man prays for the salvation of others, he is clearly praying for the will of God (II Pet. 3:9). If an obedient Christian prays for the salvation of a lost person, he can confidently expect that man's eventual conversion (Matt. 7:7).

In addition to praying for the conversion of the lost, the soul-winner should pray for himself and the evangelistic efforts of others. Paul asked the Ephesians to pray that he would proclaim the gospel boldly (Eph. 6:18-20). He urged the Colossians to pray that he would have opportunities to witness (Col. 4:2-3). He also asked the Thessalonians to pray for the spread of the gospel through him and for protection from those who would oppose it (II Thess. 3:1-2). The Lord Jesus exhorts us to pray for Him to burden the hearts of Christians to become faithful witnesses because the fields are ready for the harvest (Matt. 9:37-38).

God works through His Spirit. The lost are in a desperate condition; their minds are utterly darkened to the gospel (II Cor. 4:4). They cannot receive spiritual truth (I Cor. 2:14). They are unable to help themselves out of their spiritual death (Eph. 2:1), and by themselves they can demonstrate no desire toward the things of God (John 6:44). Only the Holy Spirit's work in the heart of a sinner can draw a man to Christ.

As the gospel is preached, the Spirit of God works mightily in the heart of the lost man. He convicts him of the sin of unbelief and convinces him of the true nature of Christ and the certainty of judgment (John 16:8-11). He enlightens his mind to the truth (John 1:9; Acts 26:18; Eph. 1:18; Heb. 6:4-9) and draws him to Christ (John 12:32). God will not force a man to be saved, but no

Doing Our Part
Prayer, like verbal witnessing, is part of the "divine/human endeavour." Consequently, just praying for someone to be saved does not guarantee his salvation any more than just witnessing guarantees salvation. However, both prayer and witnessing are our responsibilities. See Romans 10:1.

understand it in the right away.

12: Sure enough, verse 12 shows that she was skeptical of this Jewish man. She thought He was making a boast of some mystical power. If the great patriarch Jacob had to dig a well, how could this modern Jew have other water?

13-14: With His next assertion the Lord succinctly showed the inadequacy of Jacob's water, made Himself the object of the woman's spiritual interest, and revealed that His "water"

had the spiritual meaning of *eternal life*. This level of skill at turning a conversation may seem far beyond anything average people can attain. But remember two facts: first, even humanly speaking, the Lord had years of practice at personal evangelism; second, the same ever-present Lord is the One who miraculously turns sinners to salvation even when we do the talking.

15: This verse indicates that the woman still took Jesus' words in a literal sense,

just as Nicodemus did in 3:4. Constantly flowing water sounded like a convenient magic trick that would have saved her a lot of walking and carrying.

16-18: Once he had her interest and had lowered her defensiveness, Christ confronted her with the most offensive part of the gospel. A free gift sounds good to anyone. The hard part comes for every human when he must admit he has offended God and repent of his personal guilt and sinfulness. Confession

one can blame God if a man rejects the truth and goes to hell. God works through His Spirit to help lost men gain life through Christ.

God works through you. As a Christian, you may wonder why God did not take you home to heaven immediately after you were saved. The answer may be found in Christ's high-priestly prayer in John 17. The Lord prayed on behalf of believers, "I pray not that thou shouldest take them out of the world, but that thou shouldest keep them from the evil. They are not of the world, even as I am not of the world. Sanctify them through thy truth: thy word is truth. As thou hast sent me into the world, even so have I also sent them into the world" (vv. 15-18). We would be able to praise and fellowship with God more effectively in heaven; however, there are no lost souls in heaven. God has left believers in this world in order to reach lost souls for Him. Witnessing to others is an important aspect of our service to Christ.

29

---

and repentance are necessary affronts to natural human pride. This is the point at which many people will reject the gospel.

We cannot tell what Samaritan laws about divorce were on the books at this time. Among contemporary Jews, divorce was a legal practice. Apparently there was no limit to the number of possible marriages (Matthew 19:3-7; Mark 10:2-4). The Lord used His omniscience to show that He knew all about her sinful lifestyle.

Application: Although we may not have the power to recite a person's particular sins in this manner, we know from Scripture that everyone we face is a sinner before God. We depend on the Lord Himself to expose sin. Once again, it is the Lord who does the supernatural work of drawing men to Himself even when we are His spokesmen.

19-20: The woman perceived that this Jew had supernatural insight. Her question was over an ongoing point of dissension between Jews and Samaritans. It was not merely a theologically abstract question either; the two nations blasted each other for heresy. The place of true worship was a volatile issue. The Samaritan probably wanted to deflect the conversation from her sinful lifestyle.

21: "Woman" was a term of courteous

Review Questions

1. What single word in the following verse indicates the Christian's relationship to lost people?

   "Now then we are ambassadors for Christ, as though God did beseech you by us: we pray you in Christ's stead, be ye reconciled to God" (II Cor. 5:20).

   "ambassadors"

2. Why did you pick that word?

   An ambassador is someone sent as a messenger from one kingdom to another. Paul calls us ambassadors because God sends us with a message to the lost world.

3. Why is Matthew 13:3-9 more appropriately called the Parable of the Soils than the Parable of the Sower?

   The concept of soils conveys Christ's intended message—the different ways people respond to the gospel. The sower is incidental to the story.

4. List five works the Spirit of God performs in the heart of a lost man.

   1) Convicts him of the sin of unbelief
   2) Convinces him of the true nature of Christ
   3) Convinces him of the certainty of judgment
   4) Enlightens his mind to the truth
   5) Draws him to Christ

30

---

respect. The debate between Jews and Samaritans was over the place of worship. While Jews held that the Jerusalem temple was the right place, Samaritans believed it was their Mt. Gerizim. Jesus caught her off guard by simply telling the truth; soon, he told her, it will not matter at what geographic location people worship God.

Application: Jesus refused to follow a tangent into theological dispute. Do not allow people to waste your time endlessly arguing points of conflict. As with this woman, contentious people usually just want to deflect attention from their sin.

22: Jesus drew a clear distinction between Jews and Samaritans, both identifying Himself as a Jew and asserting that the Jews possessed the real truth. Samaritans rejected the authority of the History Books, Wisdom Books, Psalms, Major Prophets, and Minor Prophets. However, the Samaritans did accept the Pentateuch. Thus, they worshiped the true God without knowing what He was really like.

23: The Lord referred to the new era He was initiating in which genuine spiritual worship would replace the ritualized worship at the temple. Worshiping God "in spirit" had always been the right way to worship Him, but Jesus focused on the revival of proper worship that His earthly life and ministry would bring.

_F_ 5. God uses humans as witnesses because He speaks to sinners only through a mediator.

_F_ 6. Praying for specific people to be saved is unnecessary because God wants everyone to be saved.

Which option in each of the following two sets is not one of the "teachings in the New Testament that emphasize the supreme importance of evangelizing the lost"?

_D_ 7.

    A. Christ told us to witness.
    B. Christ expects us to witness.
    C. Our witnessing shows we are really saved.
    D. Christ promised us many people would believe the gospel.

_B_ 8.

    A. Witnessing shows we are not ashamed of Christ.
    B. Christ never turns away sinners we bring to Him.
    C. Christ gave us the Holy Spirit to help us.
    D. Christ witnessed to lost people.

After each paragraph below identify which type of soil most likely represents the person described. Explain why you chose each answer.

You met a guy named Leopold on visitation. After hearing the gospel from you, he tearfully repented of his sin and prayed to accept Christ. He started coming to your church that week. He would show up at the youth meetings, always acting like he was having a good time. But he came only once

---

24: The verse could also be read "God is spirit." He is not one spirit among many, but He is by nature spiritual, not physical, and therefore not to be identified with a physical structure. "In spirit and in truth" refers to sincere and legitimate worship in contrast to the formalistic ceremonial worship in both Jerusalem and Gerizim.

Application: Directly challenge the person's misconceptions about God and dependence on outward religion.

What God is like is up to Him to reveal, not up to human minds to imagine. God is by nature spiritual and therefore unbound to physical places such as temples, synagogues, and church buildings. Every man and woman must deal with God personally.

25: The Samaritans had a dim idea of the Messiah from the Pentateuch. (Deuteronomy 18:18 is messianic.) The woman tried to avoid facing the meaning of Jesus' words by resorting

to a higher authority. She may not have known how to handle the Jew's uncomfortably probing statements, but the Messiah would make all things clear when He came. She felt that this Jew's words were drawing her to accept an invitation from God to a relationship on a level beyond anything her religious background had offered.

Application: Simply stating the truth can make an unsaved person aware that God wants something from him.

the following month, and then stopped coming. You went to visit him at home, but he seemed distracted. He said he has been too busy lately to come to church but promised to come again soon. After three months, he still has not come back.

__B__ 9. Leopold appears to be

    A. the way side.
    B. stony ground.
    C. thorny ground.
    D. good ground.

Explain:

His quick acceptance and emotional involvement followed by sudden lack of interest are characteristic of an impulsive person who may not have been truly converted.

You have been friends with Juanita since she joined your church over a year ago. Halfway through your senior year, Juanita became a little depressed about her family's financial situation and started diligently researching which college major brought the highest starting salary. She went to a different college than you did, and now you rarely hear from her. You found out that she is not going to any church in her college town and that she started dating an older student who doesn't seem to be a Christian.

__C__ 10. Juanita appears to be

    A. the way side.
    B. stony ground.
    C. thorny ground.
    D. good ground.

Explain:

She acted like a devoted Christian, but over time worldly cares distracted her, leading her to forsake Christian friends and pursue worldly goals.

Plainly explaining basic doctrine often leads to the question "so what?" in a person's mind. People will try to reconcile what you say with their own religion. Many people today, like the Samaritan woman, actually acknowledge Jesus Christ as a special person. With modern Jews, the Messiah is still a possible avenue of witness. Bring the person to the one vital point—Jesus of Nazareth is God in human flesh and He came to save sinners.

26: Jesus unpretentiously declared that He is the Messiah. This verse is the climax of the passage. At this point the Samaritan woman faced a simple but crucial decision: to believe or not to believe.

28-30: The woman's testimony was enough to lead some Samaritans to trust Christ (v. 39), but others trusted Him later after hearing His own teaching (vv. 41-42). This Samaritan revival demonstrated that Christ came to save all men, not just Jews, and that He is able to save everyone who comes to Him in faith.

Application: From verses 39-42 notice again the two categories of converts; one person believes quickly, but another demands deeper investigation before believing. Neither is unusual. Also notice the impact a single conversion can have. The more hardened the sinner, the more meaningful to other sinners is his transformation.

CHAPTER THREE

Following a Plan for Witnessing

Memory Verses: Luke 24:45-48

A Christian will witness clearly and thoroughly when he follows a plan. Paul exhorts, "Let all things be done decently and in order" (I Cor. 14:40). A cogent presentation is important because saving faith is based on a clear understanding of the gospel (cf. Rom. 10:17). A person must know to what or whom he is entrusting his eternal welfare. If he does not understand upon whom he is relying for salvation, then he has been misled. A misplaced or misled faith is not true saving faith.

Each witnessing opportunity brings the challenge of adapting to the particular needs of a lost person. The soulwinner must answer his questions and address his particular concerns and circumstances. Yet no matter how much the believer has to adapt his presentation, he must be sure to present the gospel clearly. Mapping out a plan for witnessing will facilitate this goal.

Maps are vital aids for finding the way to any destination. Cartography, the science of mapmaking, has been practiced since

before the birth of Christ. Babylonian maps recorded on clay tablets date back to 2300 B.C. Anaximander, a Greek mathematician, produced a map of the world around 550 B.C. Ptolemy of Alexandria (A.D. 90-168) published an eight-volume work entitled *Guide to Geography,* a resource which greatly influenced mapmaking for nearly a thousand years. Martin Waldseemuller's world map produced in 1507 was probably the first to include America. Cartography became especially important during the age of exploration, for "a newly discovered

I appreciate your uncle's attempt to draw us a map, but Ptolemy of Alexandria he's not.

33

Exercise: Soulwinning Scenarios—Witness to Each Other!

Goal: Use staged scenarios to envision different witnessing encounters and to practice reacting to unexpected challenges while witnessing to someone.

Procedure: Select three pairs of students to illustrate three different witnessing encounters. The three "Christians" have the same job in each scene—to implement the techniques they are learning for approaching a person and initiating a conversation. The three "pagans" will each be different. They represent three kinds of unsaved people.

Obtain three pieces of paper. On one write, "Teenager. Sarcastic, slightly arrogant. Likes worldly music. Idolizes sports stars. Thinks church is for children and weirdoes." On another write, "Middle-aged business professional. Polite, slightly condescending. Likes his kids and spouse. Idolizes rich people. Thinks church is for old people and weirdoes." On the last write, "Elderly person. Friendly, slightly hard of hearing. Likes children (anyone under 40). Idolizes no one. Thinks church is for hypocrites."

Give one note to each pagan and have him assume the persona described. Each pair will play out a witnessing encounter in front of the class.

place can only be systematically reached again if it has been mapped" *(Encyclopedia Americana,* 18:287).

In the spiritual realm, lost men cannot find the way to Christ without proper directions. Christians have been entrusted with the gospel and should be able to point others to Christ. A poorly drawn map causes confusion and does not provide much help in reaching a destination. In the same way, the believer must be able to present clearly the plan of salvation. The rest of this chapter provides a workable step-by-step plan for pointing others to Christ.

I. Initiate the Conversation.

The soulwinner labors for men's souls. He is a farmer who sows the seed of the Word, waters it, and reaps the spiritual harvest. He is a soldier warring against Satan, who deceives men by darkening their minds. He is an athlete striving for the victory in the race against the powers of sin, the world, and the Devil in the lives of others. These metaphors suggest that the Christian is on the offensive. The believer does not simply provide a passive, "silent" witness; he actively seeks to reach others with the gospel of Christ.

Encourage each Christian to go through the steps in starting a conversation, smoothly cover the basic facts of the gospel, and lead the pagan to a point of decision.

Grading is not necessary, though it is a way to discourage the potential levity.

Discussion: Doctrines of Salvation
Goal: Verbally give an unsaved person a doctrinally accurate gospel message that is stated in nontechnical words.

Lead your class in preparing simple and clear statements for communicating the gospel. Many unsaved people cannot understand Christian jargon. Proper forethought can make a major difference in how quickly someone comprehends what you are saying.

Elicit from the class a list of *facts* an unsaved person has to know to be saved. Ask the students these questions: What *information* will you give the person as you witness to him? How much Bible *knowledge* is necessary for salvation? If the students are reserved with their suggestions, offer more. If they are generous with their suggestions, ask them how long they think it will take to relate all of the facts to an unsaved person.

Because the New Testament regularly portrays the believer as the aggressor in the search for souls; therefore, he should seek out opportunities and, to the best of his ability, even *create* opportunities to witness for Christ. An unsaved person normally does not seek the gospel, nor does he usually initiate a conversation about spiritual matters. The believer, therefore, is responsible for presenting the gospel to others.

Build rapport. The believer can witness to someone most effectively when there is a reasonable amount of mutual trust and emotional affinity. This relationship is called *rapport* [ra•PORE]. A believer may gain rapport with someone through a previous acquaintance, common interests, or friendship. Paul understood the importance of gaining rapport with his audience. When he preached to the Athenians on Mars Hill (Acts 17:18-34), he referred to their altar erected to the "UNKNOWN GOD." Paul stated that he knew this God, and he then began to preach about Him (v. 23). The apostle also struck a common chord with the Athenians by quoting some of their poets (v. 28). It is not always easy to find common ground with someone, but it is very important in gaining an opportunity to share the gospel.

Paul also sought to build rapport with fellow Jews. He identified himself as a kinsman, and he attended the synagogue, participating in the services. He also used the Old Testament, the Jewish Scriptures, to present Christ.

Although Paul usually preached to total strangers, he tried to identify with them as much as time and circumstances allowed. He outlined his practice in I Corinthians 9:22: "I am made all things to all men, that I might by all means save some." Paul's ability to gain rapport with others usually earned him an opportunity to present Christ.

Stimulate interest. After the soulwinner builds rapport with someone, he should then look for the right moment to turn the conversation toward spiritual matters. The soulwinner may accomplish this by asking certain questions. The following questions may be used to direct the conversation toward Christ.

"Has anyone ever shown you from the Bible how to have your sins forgiven? May I show you some brief passages from the Bible that teach this truth?"

An Object Lesson
The Athenian altar to an unknown god may have been a catch-all shrine dedicated to any deity missed by the polytheistic Athenians. It may also have been devoted to a legendary god whose name was unknown. Either way, it was appropriate as an illustration of a deity whom the Athenians did not know.

A Poetry Lesson
Some have said that Paul's quotation of a secular poet shows that the Bible is not entirely God's Word. However, Paul is merely using an appropriate quotation to argue a truth about God. He does not validate everything the Greek poet wrote or elevate the poet's work to the level of Scripture. The words are Scripture because of their use by Paul, an apostle of Christ, not because of their inherent authority.

Your object is to get more information at hand than is practical so that the students can practice condensing the truths into clear, compact phrases.

Once you have gathered information, ask your class members how they would bring someone to the point of making a decision. Bringing someone to a decision is not appropriate to every witnessing situation, but it should normally be the soulwinner's goal. People are much more agreeable to listening passively to information than to making a decision. Forethought can help at this point too.

Demonstrate how several facts can be compressed into single statements. For example, suppose you and your class had collected these facts:

"The Bible says everyone is a sinner. That means you and I are both sinners."

"God is absolutely perfect. He cannot let any sin be in His presence. You have to be absolutely perfect to be in God's presence."

"You would have to commit no sin at all to live with God forever. You cannot stop sinning, but even if you could, sins you have already committed will keep you from going to heaven."

"Jesus was God's Son. He was perfect and sinless. He died on the

"Our church teaches the Bible. May I take a few minutes to show you what the primary lesson of the Bible is?"

"Most people have thought about God at some point in their lives. May I show you what the Bible teaches about knowing God in this life and in the afterlife?"

"The most important command in the Bible is to love God. May I take a few moments to show you how a person can love God according to the Bible?"

"If you were to stand before God today, do you know what you would say to gain entrance to heaven? May I show you what the Bible teaches about going to heaven?"

"Do you know what it is that God says should be the greatest influence in all of life's decisions? May I show you from Scripture what that influence is?"

"Almost everyone is interested in having a life full of peace and satisfaction. Would you be willing to let me share with you how you can obtain peace and joy from the God of the Bible?"

Obviously, the soulwinner can use other questions, but these questions demonstrate that there are many ways to turn a conversation tactfully to a presentation of the gospel. The soulwinner should ask questions that are appropriate in the context of the conversation. Also, he should make an effort to make the lost person feel at ease even if he cannot answer the question.

II. Follow an Outline.

Saving faith is based on certain basic truths of the Bible. The presentation of these truths, therefore, must be clear and complete. One way to insure that the gospel is presented clearly and completely is to use an outline. The soulwinner may follow this outline rigidly, or he may adapt it according to the particular circumstances or needs of the hearer. The following outline also provides transitional statements to allow for a smooth and logical progression between main points.

Wed.

36

cross for you so that you would not have to go to hell forever."

"You need to believe in Jesus to save you. When you accept Jesus as your personal Savior, He takes away all your sin and gives you eternal life as a free gift."

The first pair of sentences is redundant, so we can combine the two statements. The next three sentences are not always necessary, since many people's conception of God includes perfection. The next pair of sentences is somewhat clumsy and not necessary unless "sinner" is misunderstood. The sentences about the Lord Jesus actually *lack* significant information; namely, that Jesus is fully God, a much more striking and accurate piece of information. The final pair of sentences is imprecise. The wording could sound jargonish to some people. More precise English words like "trust" and less wordy sentences would make the meaning clearer.

This activity will require some on-the-spot thinking, but there is no single best answer. Also, all students will have different mental images of people they are witnessing to; consequently, each will have different ideas about what an unsaved person should hear and how forcefully one should state the gospel.

Though you may rearrange some material and include additional material,

I. Who is God?

A. He is a loving Savior.

The Bible teaches in I John 4:8 and 16 that God's very nature is love. He is controlled by a willingness to sacrifice Himself for the spiritual good of man. The Scriptures also teach in John 3:16 that God's love is extended to all men through the sacrificial death of His Son, Jesus Christ. Second Corinthians 13:11 states that those who trust Christ as Savior will have the God of love dwelling with them.

1.
2.
3.

B. He is a just judge.

No one respects a judge who hands down sentences that contradict the law. Naturally, men would lose all respect for God if He did not remain fair by rewarding good and punishing evil. Psalm 75:7 teaches that God is the judge of all men. He will always judge accurately and fairly, as Genesis 18:25 and Psalm 96:10 teach. Hebrews 9:27 says that "it is appointed unto men once to die, but after this the judgment." After a man dies, he becomes subject to judgment.

C. He is Lord over all.

God created all things and therefore owns all things. That ownership gives Him the right to control all things and expect His creatures to submit to Him. Colossians 1:16 says, "For by him were all things created, that are in heaven, and that are in earth, visible and invisible, whether they be thrones, or dominions, or principalities, or powers: all things were created by him, and for him."

For a man to ignore or rebel against God is a sin that will bring eternal consequences. Paul warns, "Nay but, O man, who art thou that repliest against God? Shall the thing formed say to him that formed it, Why hast thou made me thus? Hath not the potter power over the clay, of the same lump to make one vessel unto honour, and another unto dishonour?" (Rom. 9:20-21). Christ is Lord over all; He deserves our loyalty and obedience.

Transition: God loves man and wants to show him kindness, but He is just and cannot overlook man's sin.

37

Tract Analysis
You may want to compare this outline to some of the tracts your students are using in their class project. Show the students that they can use this outline to measure a tract's thoroughness and doctrinal content.

Why Does Sin Exist?
It may be necessary to deal with the problem of why God allowed sin to enter the world at all if He is all-powerful. There is no fully satisfying answer to this question. We can observe only that

1. Man can love God freely only if it is also possible for him to reject God.

2. God punishes all sin through physical and eternal death.

3. God did all the work necessary for salvation, desires and commands everyone to be saved, and saves everyone who wants to be saved.

Christ the Creator
Colossians 1:16 specifically refers to Christ. This verse proves that God the Son as well as God the Father acted in Creation.

---

the following is an example of a concise statement of the gospel:

1. You are a sinner and cannot save yourself.

2. The Lord Jesus Christ as God in a human body took all the punishment for your sins when He died on the cross; He also showed His ability to give you eternal life when He rose from the dead.

3. If you will repent of your sin and trust Christ to save you, He will.

Discussion: Dealing with Different People

Goal: Learn from three encounters in the Book of Acts what the Lord expects in personal evangelism.

For each of the following incidents, summarize the background to the story and read the most relevant portions of Scripture in class. Emphasize that the

Lord gave us these stories as our pattern to follow in spreading the gospel. God shows *supernatural* control in each case, signifying that each was part of His plan to complete the New Testament. We want to focus on two *natural* features of these three passages: the content of the gospel message and the background of the person saved.

What is man's problem?

Man is guilty because of his sin nature.

Every man is bound to sin because he has sin in his heart. Men are born this way. Just as a dog acts like a dog, a pig behaves like a pig, and a snake writhes and strikes like a snake, so man acts like a sinner because it is in his nature to sin. Psalm 51:5 and Romans 5:12 teach this truth.

Man is guilty because of his sinful acts.

Man is condemned by God not only because he has a sinful nature but also because he has performed sinful deeds. Every man has entertained sinful thoughts and committed acts that make him worthy of condemnation. Romans 3:23 says, "For all have sinned, and come short of the glory of God."

Man is separated from God because of sin.

According to Habakkuk 1:13, God abhors the sight of evil. Sin causes a great separation between God and man. Isaiah taught, "But your iniquities have separated between you and your God, and your sins have hid his face from you, that he will not hear" (59:2). By sinning, man has earned spiritual death (separation from God) and physical death for himself. Romans 6:23 speaks of the consequences of man's sin.

Transition: How can a man solve his problem of sin? He must come to Christ, who conquered sin on the cross.

38

1. Philip and the Ethiopian—Acts 8:26-40

The content of the gospel in this case appears in verses 32 and 35. The Ethiopian was reading Isaiah 53, a prophecy of Christ's suffering and death in the place of sinners. When Philip explained the passage, he "preached unto him [the Ethiopian] Jesus." Jesus is the message of the Old Testament as much as the New. The only message a sinner needs to hear is the person and work of Jesus Christ.

The background of the person converted—

Nationality: African (Ethiopian)
Class: High nobility, wealthy, and influential

2. Peter and Cornelius—Acts 10:34-43

Peter summarized the gospel message in verses 38-43. He affirmed the Lord's power and goodness (v. 38), unjust death (v. 39), resurrection (v. 40), humanity (v. 41), ultimate judgment of all mankind (v. 42), and offer of salvation to all who believe (v. 43). Notice that he did not explicitly refer to the Old Testament but did cite its broad support in verse 43.

[handwritten: Title]

III. What has God done?

A. Christ has become the God-man.

Jesus Christ is God; yet He came to earth in human flesh. This is the meaning of the apostle John's words, "The Word [Christ] was made flesh, and dwelt among us" (John 1:14). Christ was the fulfillment of Isaiah's prophecy recorded in Matthew 1:23, "Behold, a virgin shall be with child, and shall bring forth a son, and they shall call his name Emmanuel, which being interpreted is, God with us." As God, Christ possessed all the eternal power and purity of God. He alone could accomplish the miracle of salvation for man.

B. Christ has lived a perfect life.

Had Christ been a sinner like other men, He could not have died for the sins of mankind. The New Testament clearly teaches that no one can legitimately accuse Christ of having committed a sin (II Cor. 5:21). He was tempted in every way possible, but He never yielded to temptation (Heb. 4:15).

C. Christ bore our sins and their penalty on the cross.

The apostle Peter wrote that Christ bore our sins while He hung on the cross (I Pet. 2:21-24). He suffered there for us so that we would not have to experience the wrath of God in hell forever. He was our propitiation; in other words, He bore God's wrath in our stead (I John 2:1-2).

D. Christ rose from the grave as proof of His victory over sin and death.

The resurrection of Christ is part of the good news of salvation (I Cor. 15:4). Speaking of the Lord Jesus, Paul wrote, "Who was delivered for our offences, and was raised again for our justification" (Rom. 4:25). The resurrection of Christ was part of the great saving act of God on behalf of sinful men.

[handwritten margin notes: 1. scriptures refs 2. Work of salvation belief/repentance]

The Infinite Christ
Christ's infinite capacity allowed Him to suffer in one moment all the punishment that would take us, with our limited capacity, an infinite amount of time to undergo.

It is important to observe that within the Bible there are different ways to present the gospel. None is exhaustive because it takes the whole New Testament (if not the whole Bible) to say everything necessary about Christ.

The background of the person converted—

Nationality: European (Italian; Acts 10:1)

Class: Respected career soldier

3. Paul and the Jailer—Acts 16:25-34

As recorded, the content of the gospel was very brief this time. However, verse 32 indicates that Paul and Silas probably taught the jailer much more. The author of Acts (Luke) did not find it necessary to record every word. Paul spoke the same message that had been recorded earlier in the Gospels and the first part of Acts.

The background of the person converted—

Nationality: European (Greek)

Class: Working class—jailers were apparently poor men of low social standing.

In conclusion, draw your class's attention to the fact that each passage also involved a different witness. Philip, Peter, and Paul were very different men, but God used them all to lead

Because Christ rose from the dead, the believer has the promise that one day his body will be resurrected and that he will live forever in the presence of God (I Cor. 15:54-57). This is the greatest of all benefits of faith in Christ.

Transition: Christ has borne sin and its penalty for all men. However, men are not automatically free from their sins. The work of Christ on the cross is effective only for those who personally accept Christ as Lord and Savior.

IV. What must man do?

Man must turn from his sin.

Turning from the control and love of sin at conversion is called repentance. **Repentance** involves both turning from the controlling influence of sin and turning to God (I Thess. 1:9-10).

Man must place his confidence in Christ.

Saving faith is not merely the *knowledge* that Jesus is the Savior and Lord of all; even the demons *understand* certain truths about God (James 2:19). True faith is a careful, thorough decision to trust what Christ did on the cross and what He teaches in the Bible (Luke 14:27-33).

The one who believes in Christ decides to rely on Christ as his Savior from the penalty and power of sin. He also places his faith in God to guide and control his life. True faith results in salvation from sin. Acts 16:31 states, "Believe on the Lord Jesus Christ, and thou shalt be saved."

III. Conclude with an Invitation.

Ask the lost person if he understands your presentation. As the believer presents the gospel to a lost person, the Holy Spirit

people to Christ. Finally, state again that each convert was from a different background and station in life. God sends His messengers to people of every rank in society.

will begin to work in the sinner's heart and mind. Second Corinthians 4:6 says, "For God, who commanded the light to shine out of darkness, hath shined in our hearts, to give the light of the knowledge of the glory of God in the face of Jesus Christ." Few things in life are as amazing to behold as the Lord's enlightening the mind of an unbeliever and making him receptive to the gospel. A scriptural example of the Holy Spirit's working is Lydia of Thyatira, who was converted to Christ while visiting Philippi. Luke recounts this incident in Acts 16:14, "And a certain woman named Lydia, a seller of purple, of the city of Thyatira, which worshipped God, heard us: whose heart the Lord opened, that she attended unto the things which were spoken of Paul."

The Scriptures clearly teach that God is at work in the mind of an unbeliever while the truth is being presented. However, this fact does not lessen the believer's responsibility to present the truth in a clear and interesting way. Colossians 4:6 exhorts, "Let your speech be alway with grace, seasoned with salt, that ye may know how ye ought to answer every man."

In addition to presenting the message clearly, the soulwinner should make sure that the hearer has understood the presentation. Remember that one of Satan's devices to keep men in the bondage of sin is confusion about the truth. Jesus taught in Matthew 13:19, "When any one heareth the word of the kingdom, and understandeth it not, then cometh the wicked one, and catcheth away that which was sown in his heart." The soulwinner must remember that "God is not the author of confusion, but of peace, as in all churches of the saints" (I Cor. 14:33).**Encourage an immediate decision for Christ.** Peter wrote, "The Lord is not slack concerning his promise, as some men count slackness; but is longsuffering to usward, not willing that any should perish, but that all should come to repentance" (II Pet. 3:9). God wants the unsaved person to turn from sin and trust in Christ. In the mind of God, now is the best time for a person to be saved. Second Corinthians 6:2 says, "For he saith, I have heard thee in a time accepted, and in the day of salvation have I succoured thee: behold, now is the accepted time; behold, now is the day of salvation."

Reinforcement

Discuss with your class some improper methods of compelling a person to confess Christ. You could range from the ridiculous—such as holding a gun to his head or writing him a check—to more subtle errors—such as appealing excessively to his sense of guilt or acting like you will not leave him alone until he prays the sinner's prayer.

Discussion: Making It Plain

Goal: Clarify the gospel to someone who initially fails to grasp the message of salvation.

Discuss with your class ways to help a person who does not understand the gospel after the first time you explain it. For example, suggest to the students that a first-time hearer of the gospel might not be familiar with all the language that a soulwinner uses. Tell the students to be careful about using Christian jargon. Phrases like "accept Jesus as Savior" and "just rest in Jesus" might be misunderstood if not carefully explained. Likewise, be careful to explain Bible words such as *repent, justification,* or *redeemed* when you use them.

Sometimes people need illustrations or word pictures in order to grasp the concepts. Teach your class some simple ways to visualize the gospel. For instance, the concept of grace (salvation

The soulwinner may want to ask the lost person one of the following questions to bring him to a point of salvation.

"Would you like to pray now and receive the gift of eternal life through faith in Christ?"

"Since you understand the good news about Christ and His salvation, would you like to accept Him now as your Savior from sin?"

"Would you like to decide now to become a follower of Christ by trusting in His death and resurrection for you?"

The believer must be cautious about his use of logic and persuasion at this point. He is encouraging the lost person to make the most important decision of his life. A relationship with Christ must not be entered into lightly, and the unsaved person must realize the seriousness of his choice. He must make his choice willingly, not because he is coerced. The soulwinner can always rest in the truth of I Corinthians 3:6: "I have planted, Apollos watered; but God gave the increase." The Christian witness should never stoop to desperate, carnal techniques to pressure someone into making a decision for Christ.

Offer an opportunity to call on the Lord for salvation. A person does not receive salvation simply by repeating a prayer. Salvation is a choice to trust Christ as Savior and Lord for the rest of one's life. This choice occurs in the heart or inner man. However, the Scriptures teach that out of the fullness of the heart the mouth speaks (Matt. 12:34), and prayer is an appropriate expression of the heart. This association is so close that the Scriptures seem to link calling on the Lord with salvation itself. Romans 10:12-13 states, "For the same Lord over all is rich unto all that call upon him. For whosoever shall call upon the name of the Lord shall be saved."

It is a good practice to encourage the lost person to pray aloud rather than silently; articulating one's thoughts often gives more meaning and clarity to them. This prayer should include a statement of trust in Christ as Savior and a statement of allegiance to follow Christ as God, rejecting sin and self as the rulers of life.

42

is given freely to the undeserving) may be illustrated by giving the person a dollar (or a tract if you prefer) and then protesting that since he did nothing to earn that dollar, he should not have it. Obviously, he has it because you gave it to him, not because he earned it. All such illustrations are ultimately inadequate, but they can serve to clarify certain points in an unsaved person's mind.

Conclusion

As you establish your priorities in life, consider the words of Dr. C. I. Scofield, a man of great missionary fervor and soulwinning zeal, and the editor of America's most loved study Bible, the Scofield Reference Bible.

"Let us leave the government of the world till the King comes. Let us leave the civilizing of the world to be an incidental effect of the presence there of the gospel of Christ. Let us give our time, our strength, our money, our days to make Christ known to every creature" (*Knight's Illustrations for Today,* p. 318).

This statement should express the sentiment of every Christian heart. There are other important priorities in the Christian life, but nothing is more crucial than proclaiming the gospel to the lost in a clear, interesting, and persuasive manner.

Analysis of Questions

1. Acts 17:18 is the first verse of a passage that teaches the importance of rapport, but the verse itself does not deal with rapport building.

__D__ 1. Which verse most clearly shows the importance of building rapport?

   A. I Corinthians 14:40
   B. Romans 10:17
   C. Acts 17:18
   D. I Corinthians 9:22

__B__ 2. Imagine that you just finished witnessing to a person, but he is reluctant to pray to the Lord for salvation at that moment. Which of these represents a proper response?

   A. "That's fine, you can get saved any time you want under any circumstances. Don't hurry."

   B. "I don't want to push you into anything, but please remember that the Bible says in II Corinthians 6:2, 'Now is the accepted time, behold now is the day of salvation.'"

   C. "Come on, you pagan, you need to do it NOW!"

   D. "Why don't you understand? It should be obvious that the plain facts of the case demand that you get saved now."

Imagine that you ask a person whether he understands what you have just presented to him and he responds with one of the statements in the next three questions. In the blank beside each question, write "T" if the statement reflects a proper understanding of the gospel and "F" if it indicates a misconception.

___F___ 3. "What you are saying is I have to switch over to your church if I want to get saved?"

___T___ 4. "What you are saying is I have to ask Jesus to forgive all my sins all at once and to make me a Christian?"

___F___ 5. "What you are saying is I have to love Jesus to get to heaven?"

Short/Long Answer

For the next four sentences, consult the sample outline for witnessing. Give the main point and subpoint along with the Scripture reference that would be the right thing to say next if the person to whom you are witnessing were to say the following:

6. "Do you think God sends people to hell? I just don't see how a loving God could send people to hell!"

Who is God?
He is just.
Genesis 18:25

7. "I'm not perfect, of course, but I don't really do anything bad."

What is man's problem?
Man is guilty because of his sinful acts.
Romans 3:23

8. "I know Jesus is a great teacher, and I think it is terrible He was killed, but what does He have to do with me?"

What has God done?
Christ bore our sins and their penalty on the cross.
I Peter 2:21-24

9. "You'll want me to give up drugs if I get saved, right?"

What must man do?
Man must turn from his sin.
I Thessalonians 1:9-10

5. A saved person will love Jesus, but "loving Jesus" is not the gospel, especially with the ambiguity of the English word *love*. The gospel requires repentance and faith.

6-9. It is possible to think of other points in the outline to counter these objections. However, you should show your students that these are the best answers because they directly meet the objections.

45

10. From the principles you learned in this chapter, explain why questions are appropriate for turning a conversation toward spiritual matters.

    Acceptable answers include the following: Questions allow a natural transition, making the person feel as if he turned the conversation himself. Questions are more tactful and less confrontational than blunt statements. They evoke thoughtful interaction from the person.

CHAPTER FOUR

Laying the Foundations for Discipleship

④

Memory Verse: Colossians 1:28

In this chapter, we begin the study of the second part of disciple making, personal discipleship. After you lead someone to trust Christ, you start teaching him the things a Christian must know. You may also meet someone who, although he has been saved for a while, never had this basic instruction. Even though you did not lead him to Christ, you have the privilege of personally teaching him the basics of the Christian faith.

On the other hand, you may want to set up a Bible study with someone who is not saved in order to lead him to Christ. Some people who do not trust Christ on first hearing the gospel still want to learn more. Like Nicodemus, they want time to study the Bible and think through it for themselves. Leading such a person through a self-study course is a great way to deal with questions systematically and to provide a summary of what the Bible teaches.

To gain a new skill, you have to practice it. We are going to practice the skill of discipleship in two ways: first, by putting you in the role of a new Christian taking a basic course; second, by allowing you to lead another Christian through the same course. By first being the learner, you can work on mastering the material you will later teach. By practicing being the teacher, you will get an idea of what it will be like to hold someone accountable for the lessons, summarize the basics of Christianity in your own words, and answer another person's questions.

This chapter contains the first five lessons in James Berg's discipleship manual *Basics for Believers*. A separate copy of the booklet is included with this course for you to use to practice discipling another Christian. It covers the basics of Christianity in a simple but thorough fashion. Work through the lessons, filling in all the blanks with the most accurate answers you can devise. Remember that you will need to be able to clearly explain each answer to another person.

Objectives
Students should be able to
1. Complete five lessons in *Basics for Believers*.
2. Take the practice disciple through at least three of the same lessons.

Overview
The first chapter laid a doctrinal basis for disciple making. The second and third chapters explained the biblical and practical aspects of the first step in disciple making—personal evangelism. The last two chapters explain the principles concerning the second step in disciple making—personal discipleship.

Using *Basics for Believers* by James A. Berg as the bulk of the student text, chapters 4 and 5 seek to prepare each student to competently execute a basic personal discipleship course with a new convert.

Once a person is saved, he needs to be taught carefully and thoroughly everything about being a follower of Christ. There is no end to this process for any Christian. All of us continually learn more about being Christlike. This discipleship course would be only the beginning of a new Christian's lifetime growth in Christ.

47

Exercise

Goal: Learn what the Bible says about itself by studying Psalm 119. This study should increase the students' appreciation for the Bible and better equip them to disciple a new convert.

Introduce Psalm 119 by pointing out that it is the longest psalm, has more verses than any "chapter" in the other books of the Bible, and is the largest part of Scripture that discusses Scripture itself. It is divided into twenty-two sections of eight verses each. Each section corresponds to a successive letter of the Hebrew alphabet. Each verse within a section begins with that letter. The term for a poem whose lines start with successive letters of the alphabet is an **acrostic**, several of which occur in the Psalter. This technique may have been an aid to memorization, but it also seems to signify *completeness,* as if it is "everything from A to Z" about the subject in question.

In class, take your students through the first section of Psalm 119 (vv. 1-8) to show them how to analyze the text. Write these four categories on the board: *Descriptions of the Word of God; Petitions to God; Characteristics and Actions of the Believer; Opposites of Obeying God's Word.*

The first category is to record the different names for the Scripture used in Psalm 119. At least eight appear throughout the psalm; seven of these

Introduction

Unfortunately, many people have looked upon Christianity as just another religion. Were it not for one basic difference, this might be true. Genuine Christianity is not a religion; it is a relationship. It is a relationship with Jesus Christ.

CHRISTIANITY IS NOT A RELIGION; IT IS A RELATIONSHIP.

No one becomes a Christian by joining a church or being baptized or confirmed. One must personally know Jesus Christ (by experience) to be a Christian.

There is only one way to know Christ personally—by knowing and believing what God has told us about Him in God's Word, the Bible. In the Bible, God spells out the conditions that must be met before He accepts anyone into His family. It also tells us how to build our relationship with Him once we have become children of God.

If you are not a Christian or do not know whether you are, these simple Bible studies are for you. If you are a new Christian, these studies will help you to build your relationship with God. All you will need is some time alone, a pen or pencil, and a Bible. It is suggested that you use the Authorized Version of the Bible (the King James Version) to answer the questions. Read each verse carefully and prayerfully. Then answer the questions in your own words.

God says that the most important thing in the world is that you know Him personally. Listen to what He says in Jeremiah 9:23-24:

"Thus saith the Lord, Let not the wise man glory in his wisdom, neither let the mighty man glory in his might, let not the rich man glory in his riches: But let him that glorieth glory in this, that *he understandeth and knoweth me*" (emphasis added).

These studies can help you to "understand and know" the God of heaven.

---

occur in the first section. One or more of them are used in each of the 176 verses of the psalm.

Below is a sample result of this study. There is room for some variation in answers, but this list summarizes the key information.

A. *Descriptions of the Word of God:* law (v. 1), testimonies (v. 2), ways (v. 3), precepts (v. 4), statutes (vv. 5 and 8), commandments (v. 6), judgments (v. 7).

B. *Petitions to God:* direct my ways to keep your statutes (v. 5); forsake me not utterly (v. 8).

C. *Characteristics and Actions of the Believer:* blessed (vv. 1 and 2), seeks God with the whole heart (v. 2), walks in His ways (v. 3), commanded to keep precepts diligently (v. 4), not ashamed (v. 6), praises God with uprightness of heart (v. 7), keeps God's statutes (v. 8).

D. *Opposites of Obeying God's Word:* defilement (v. 1), iniquity (v. 3).

Have your students read one verse at a time to you, suggesting entries for each category. After you have finished all eight verses, go through each category and draw a conclusion and application for all Christians.

For example, *law, commandments,* and *judgments* point to the fact that God is the supreme Ruler and Judge, who has the right to dictate our lives. Therefore

Eternal Life–Accepting God's Gift

People today are constantly making big promises. Television advertisements promise everything from cleaner dishes to smoother-riding cars. All of these promises are trivial, however, when compared to the promise of eternal life that God offers to man.

It is sad that not every man has this eternal life. God's Word says that there are two groups of people in this world.

1. According to I John 5:11-12, what are these two groups?

   a. *They that have the Son*
   b. *They that do not have the Son*

2. What determines whether a person has eternal life (I John 5:12)?

   Whether he has the Son

3. The Bible says that all men are sinners. In Romans 3:23 God declares that "all have sinned, and come short of the glory of God." Every man has broken God's law and deserves God's punishment. The Bible says that "the wages of sin is death" (Rom. 6:23). Even though man deserves to be punished for his sin, what did God do (John 3:16)?

   God gave His only Son so that whoever believes in Him will have eternal life.

4. Can a person do anything on his own to have eternal life (Titus 3:5)?

   No

5. What must a person do to become part of God's family and have eternal life (John 1:12)?

   Receive Christ by believing on His name.

6. If a person truly desires to receive Christ and have eternal life, what will be his attitude toward sin (Isa. 55:7*a*)?

   He will hate it and be willing to forsake it.

---

we should acknowledge His right to tell us what to do.

Statutes and *precepts* show that the specifics of the law are important, so it is important that we invest time studying them to be acutely aware of God's desires for our lives.

Testimonies and *ways* indicate that God fully keeps His own law. In fact, the law is a reflection of God's character. Therefore, we look on every command as a chance to imitate God and Christ. Furthermore, we can see in the perfect law how far short of God's standard we fall and how great a gift God gives us in the imputed righteousness of Christ.

The petitions are models we can follow directly. For instance, you might have a student lead the class in prayer, asking for the same things as the psalmist. The petitions show the need for God to make us conform to His law, to give us the very ability to do what He says.

The characteristics and actions of the believer are also ours to imitate. Note especially the importance of seeking with the *whole heart*. These words mean that keeping the law takes a commitment of all our mental and spiritual strength. Obeying God is therefore not just a part-time endeavor, but a lifelong quest.

Note: A person who genuinely wants to be saved will express an attitude of repentance toward his sin. This means that he will not only acknowledge his sin (confess it to God), but also he will be sorry enough about it that he will turn away from it.

7. What does God say about a person who has not received Christ and repented of his sin (John 3:18)?

   He is condemned.

8. Is it possible for a person to know whether he has eternal life? (I John 5:13)

   Yes

9. Can you personally say, without hesitation, that you have God's gift of eternal life?

   Answers will vary.

10. If you answered yes to question 9 above, what reason(s) can you give for your answer?

    Answers will vary.

For additional study about accepting God's gift of eternal life, see John 3:1-21.

Assurance–Believing God's Promises

Once a person repents of his sin and accepts God's gift of eternal life, Satan will begin to intimidate him and will try to cast doubts in his mind. This can be expected since Jesus called Satan the "father" of lies (John 8:44). Read the following promises carefully and note what God has said He will do when a person asks Christ to save him.

"He that believeth on the Son hath everlasting life: and he that believeth not the Son shall not see life; but the wrath of God abideth on him" (John 3:36).

"And I give unto them eternal life; and they shall never perish, neither shall any man pluck them out of my hand" (John 10:28).

Discussion

Goal: Understand the long-term nature of a discipling relationship.

From the time your students begin approaching people with the gospel, they should look at witnessing as the beginning of an open-ended process by which the Lord brings a man or woman to know Himself. The basic discipleship course is only the first mutual activity in a new friendship that lasts as long as the Lord makes the relationship possible.

Discuss with your students different ways in which God can bring someone to grow as a Christian. This might be a good time to share personal testimonies of how the Lord taught someone a particular spiritual lesson. Everyone attains Christian maturity in a different way. Bring your students to understand that they cannot tell what the Lord may have planned for the person they disciple. They may or may not get to see that person grow much in Christ, but they must realize the

Lord can use any number of ways to make the disciple a mature Christian in the future.

"Him that cometh to me I will in no wise cast out" (John 6:37b).

1. A lack of assurance can be an indication that you are not trusting God's promises. Have you ever repented of your sin and asked God to save you?

   Is it possible for God to lie or go back on a promise (Titus 1:2)?

   No

   If God cannot lie and you have asked Christ to save you, what does John 5:24 say about you?

   I have everlasting life.

2. A lack of assurance can also mean that there is sin in your life that you have not confessed to God. It stands between you and God. What does Proverbs 28:13 say about the man who harbors sin in his life?

   He shall not prosper.

   If you have truly trusted Christ, you will forsake your sin; but should you sin, it is not necessary that you be saved again. You are already a member of God's family. He does not throw you out of the family, but He is disappointed and grieved over your sin. What does I John 1:9 say you are to do when you sin?

   Confess my sin

   What does this verse say that God will do?

   Forgive my sin and cleanse me from unrighteousness

After you are saved, you begin to receive greater assurance as you see certain evidences in your life. Look up these verses below and note the evidences they describe.

1. Romans 8:16–The Holy Spirit bears witness to my spirit. The Holy Spirit assures you, **"You are my child."**

2. I John 4:19–You find that you love **God.**

51

Reinforcement

Help your students see that the important question to settle regarding their salvation is not whether they remember a specific date and time they were saved. The important question is, "Do you know you are saved *now?*" However you answer that question, the thing to do is to trust Christ now. The point is that you know you are saved by what you know right now, not something you remember. This concept does not mean you can lose your salvation but that the assurance of salvation lies in *present facts,* not memory of past experiences.

3. I John 3:14—You find that you love **the brethren (God's people).**

4. John 14:27—God gives you **peace.**

5. According to II Corinthians 5:17, what should be happening to your old desires and ways? **They should be passing away.**

6. Galatians 5:17—What is going on inside you now? **There is a struggle between the flesh and the Spirit.**

Each of these evidences indicates that you are God's child. They will grow as you feed daily on God's Word. To help you resist the doubts that Satan will send your way, memorize the verses on assurance from the "Memory Verses" page in the Additional Helps for Christian Growth section in the back of this book.

If after you have studied this chapter you still do not have a real assurance of your salvation, read and reread I John 5:11-13. Then study through the first chapter of this book again and seek the help of another believer who is sure that he is saved. God desires that you feel secure in His family.

God's Word–Listening to God Speak

The Bible is a revelation of God's instructions to man. Since God Himself is the author, His Word possesses absolute authority over man. It touches on every area of life. Jesus said, "Man shall not live by bread alone, but by every word that proceedeth out of the mouth of God" (Matt. 4:4).

There are countless benefits to be gained from reading and studying God's Word.

1. *It is the source of the believer's faith.*

   "Faith cometh by hearing, and hearing by the word of God" (Rom. 10:17).

2. *It cleanses us as we obey it.*

   "Now ye are clean through the word which I have spoken unto you" (John 15:3).

"Wherewithal shall a young man cleanse his way? by taking heed thereto according to thy word" (Ps. 119:9).

3. *It gives us direction and understanding.*

"Thy word is a lamp unto my feet, and a light unto my path" (Ps. 119:105).

"The entrance of thy words giveth light; it giveth understanding to the simple" (Ps. 119:130).

4. *It gives victory over Satan when we apply it.*

"Thy word have I hid in mine heart, that I might not sin against thee" (Ps. 119:11).

Many other things can be said about the Bible. Read the following questions and look up the answers in your Bible.

1. The Bible was written over a period of sixteen centuries by some forty men, yet all sixty-six books bear a remarkable unity. They teach the same salvation and the same moral standards, and they all point to the same Savior. Who guided the writers so that they all agree (II Pet. 1:21)?

The Holy Spirit

Note: This divine guidance of what the writers recorded is called *inspiration.*

2. What two statements about the Bible are given in II Timothy 3:16?

   a. **Given by God's inspiration**
   b. **Profitable**

3. What must we do to make the Bible personally beneficial (II Tim. 2:15)?

Study it.

4. What should be our attitude toward the Bible (Ps. 119:97)?

We should love it!

5. Job considered God's Word to be the most important thing in his life. How do we know this (Job 23:12*b*)?

He calls it more important than life's necessities.

6. Why is it so important for new Christians to begin reading and studying the Bible right away (I Pet. 2:2)?

They need to grow.

For additional study about listening to God speak, see Luke 8:4-15. Read through "A Plan for a Daily Quiet Time with God" in the Additional Helps for Christian Growth section. This will give you some help in setting up a daily time of Bible reading and application for your life.

Temptation–Resisting God's Enemy

A recently saved Indian chief was asked by a missionary how things were going in his new faith. The chief replied that he felt as if two dogs were fighting inside. The black dog wanted him to do evil, and the white dog wanted him to do right. When asked by the missionary which dog was winning, the chief replied, "The dog I feed the most."

The apostle Paul wrote of this same struggle when he said, "the flesh lusteth [sets its desires] against the Spirit, and the Spirit against the flesh: and these are contrary the one to the other: so that ye cannot do the things that ye would" (Gal. 5:17).

After a person becomes a Christian, he finds that God's Spirit is continually prompting him to do right. At the same time, Satan, God's enemy, tries harder to tempt the believer to sin. Thus a continual and fierce battle rages. God's plan for overcoming Satan is set forth in the Bible. Study the following passages carefully to learn how to resist Satan.

Photodisc, Inc.

1. What description of Satan is given in I Peter 5:8?

A roaring, hungry lion

2. Hebrews 2:14 says that Christ rendered him powerless who "had the power of death, that is, the devil." Since Satan is a defeated enemy, what does God want us to be (Rom. 8:37)?

   Conquerors

3. The first battleground for most conflicts is the mind. What is a Christian to do when evil thoughts arise (II Cor. 10:5)?

   Bring them captive into obedience to Christ.

4. James 4:7 gives a two-fold plan for victory over Satan. List the two elements of this plan.

   a. ***Submit to God***
   b. ***Resist the Devil***

5. How did Jesus "resist the devil" (Matt. 4:4, 7, 10)?

   He quoted appropriate Scripture.

6. What did Jesus tell His disciples to do to resist Satan's temptations (Matt. 26:41)?

   Watch and pray

7. Besides not allowing you to be tempted past your level of endurance, what does God promise to do for you (I Cor. 10:13)?

   Provide a way of escape

8. What "way of escape" is described in II Timothy 2:22*a*?

   Fleeing lust

9. If you should fail to resist the Devil or fail to take the way of escape and find that you have sinned, what should you do (I John 1:9)?

   Confess your sin to God so He can forgive you.

10. Read Psalm 139:23-24. Take a moment to ask God to examine your heart and mind. List your areas of weakness on the following chart. Find Bible verses from "Verses for Victory" in Additional Helps for Christian Growth or find verses in

Exercise

Goal: Know what temptation to sin will be like.

Lead your class through a study of the temptation of Christ by Satan as recorded in Matthew 4:1-11. Start by observing that Satan is an intelligent being who has a strategy for tempting people to sin. Although we should not get absorbed studying demons and the occult, we must be aware of the process through which we are led into sin and how we may avoid sin's snare.

The Lord Jesus cannot sin because He is God. Stress that when Jesus was on earth no outside restraint prevented Him from yielding to temptation; rather, His own intrinsic righteousness made sin impossible. However, because he was man, Christ was subject to the weaknesses of humanity.

Emphasize the following facts to your class about the temptation: First, the Holy Spirit led Christ to the wilderness; therefore, it was ordained of God. Second, He was in a dangerous and deserted place. Compare this to Satan's temptation of Adam, who was in a perfect environment yet still failed. Third, Christ had fasted for forty days and was probably hungrier than any ordinary human has ever been. Satan attacked Christ when He was weakened.

To complete the exercise, go through the passage and point out how the other study helps and begin fortifying yourself against Satan's attacks.

Sins and Weaknesses	Verses for Victory

For additional help in resisting God's enemy, study Ephesians 6:10-18.

Prayer–Talking With God

Communication is the basis for *every* relationship. People who do not talk to each other never grow very close together. Reading the Bible and praying are the two basic activities for developing your relationship with God. Just as there are countless benefits from reading and studying God's Word, so there are untold blessings to be reaped through personal contact with God through prayer.

1. *It is the means of getting help in times of need.*

   "Let us therefore come boldly unto the throne of grace, that we may obtain mercy, and find grace to help in time of need" (Heb. 4:16).

Lord quoted an Old Testament Scripture to defeat each of Satan's attacks. Satan appealed to Christ's need for food, His need for experiences, and his need for possessions. All three are legitimate desires, but when they are satisfied outside of God's plan, these desires result in sin.

Make the application to your students. Satan will tempt them when they are physically and emotionally vulnerable. He will launch a series of temptations,

even if the first fails, and he will tempt your students to fulfill a legitimate desire in a wrong manner.

2. *It is the means of obtaining forgiveness of sins.*

"If we confess our sins, he is faithful and just to forgive us our sins, and to cleanse us from all unrighteousness" (I John 1:9).

3. *It is the means to spiritual strength.*

"Men ought always to pray, and not to faint" (Luke 18:1*b*).

4. *It makes God more real to the believer.*

"Draw nigh [near] to God, and he will draw nigh to you" (James 4:8*a*).

5. *It brings joy to the believer.*

"In thy presence is fulness of joy" (Ps. 16:11*b*).

6. *It is God's way of providing our needs.*

"Ask, and it shall be given you; seek, and ye shall find; knock, and it shall be opened unto you" (Matt. 7:7).

7. *It is God's cure for worry.*

"Be careful [worried] for nothing; but in every thing by prayer and supplication with thanksgiving let your requests be made known unto God. And the peace of God, which passeth all understanding, shall keep [guard] your hearts and minds through Christ Jesus" (Phil. 4:6-7).

God's Word is full of promises to answer our prayers. However, along with each promise is a certain condition that God wants us to meet. State the conditions described in the verses below.

1. I John 3:22

   a. **Keep His commandments.**
   b. **Do things pleasing in His sight.**

2. John 15:7

   a. **We abide in Him.**
   b. **His Word abides in us.**

57

3. John 14:13 **Ask in Jesus' name.**

4. Mark 11:24 **Believe that you will receive what you ask for.**

5. I John 5:14-15 **Ask according to His will.**

> *Note:* We will know what is "according to His will" as we study the Word of God and pray "in the Spirit" (conscious of the Holy Spirit's promptings in our hearts). The Holy Spirit helps us pray and "maketh intercession for the saints according to the will of God" (Rom. 8:26-27).

Sometimes, however, it seems that God does not hear us. Sometimes He does not answer. In either case there is a reason. Look up the following references to discover some hindrances to prayer.

1. James 4:3 **Asking out of greed or lust**
2. Isaiah 59:1-2 **Iniquities and sins**
3. Mark 11:25-26 **Failure to forgive others**

For additional help about talking with God, see Matthew 6:5-15.

Review Questions

True or False

__F__ 1. "An attitude of repentance toward sin" involves only a recognition that sin is very damaging.

__T__ 2. A truly saved person may occasionally doubt his salvation.

__F__ 3. When a new believer needs guidance from God, he should open his Bible randomly and read until a certain verse strikes him as relevant.

__T__ 4. Prayer is necessary to gain forgiveness of sin.

Multiple Choice

__B__ 5. Which of the following is not a legitimate reason for a person to believe he has eternal life?

    A. He believes God has mercy on sinners.
    B. He wants to go to heaven forever.
    C. He received Jesus Christ as his Savior.
    D. He knows Jesus died to save him from his sin.

__D__ 6. If a new convert were to tell you that he is doubting his salvation, which of the following would be a valid reason for his doubt?

    A. Satan's lies
    B. Failure to trust God's promises
    C. Unconfessed sin
    D. Each of these could be a valid reason for doubt.

Analysis of Questions

1. Repentance shows itself in sorrow and change; it is not just an acknowledgment that sin is bad.

3. This method of Bible study amounts to a mystical use of the Bible, almost as a Ouija board. The Bible is not designed to be used that way, and it is dangerous to plunge into the middle of a passage without knowing its context.

4. Confession to God requires prayer. Confession is necessary for forgiveness (I John 1:9).

5. Most people want to go to heaven, but that desire alone does not show that a person has a grasp of the gospel.

6. All three reasons appear in the section entitled "Assurance."

7. See item #3 in the section called "Temptation."

8. See the *Note* on page 58 concerning "Prayer."

9. See the introduction to the section entitled "Prayer" on page 56.

7. What is "the first battleground for most conflicts" between Satan and the Spirit of God?

   The mind

8. What member of the Trinity actually helps us pray?

   The Holy Spirit

9. What is the basis for every relationship?

   Communication

10. Suppose you reach the lesson on temptation with a disciple. He tells you that, though he believes drunkenness is sin, he is having terrible problems fighting the temptation to drink liquor. List three verses used in that lesson and write how you would apply each one to this tempted Christian's situation.

    Sample answer: II Corinthians 10:5 shows that whenever you catch yourself thinking about liquor, you need to stop and deliberately think of something else.

    James 4:7 tells us to fight against temptation and submit to doing what God wants.

    II Timothy 2:22 prohibits even going near temptation, so if you come near liquor, leave and go somewhere else.

CHAPTER FIVE

Continuing Discipleship

Memory Verses: Ephesians 4:11-13

Goals

Students should

1. Deal with the more complex problems that new converts face.
2. Develop the goal of making new converts faithful members of and participants in a good local church.

Objectives

Students should be able to

1. Complete the rest of *Basics for Believers.*
2. Take the practice disciple through at least two more of the same lessons.
3. Fulfill the class projects on passing out tracts and witnessing.

Overview

This final chapter completes our practice in the second step of disciple making, personal discipleship. The topics covered in Chapter 4 were mostly basic and unarguable. The topics in this chapter bring the possibility of more controversial discussions. The students need to be ready to face difficult issues with the people they disciple. A new Christian must eventually learn to handle hard questions in order to become a mature and stable member of the body of Christ.

Overview

Now that you have covered five basic issues in the discipleship course, we will go into topics that are more involved and more likely to cause controversy. You cannot avoid facing difficult issues with a new Christian. You should not want to avoid them; since a new Christian will have to wrestle with hard questions throughout his Christian life, he might as well learn to approach them properly from the outset.

These last three topics concern a new Christian's interaction with and influence upon other people. While Christian discipleship is never finished in this life, there is a reasonable goal for a basic discipleship course such as this one. That goal is *to make the new Christian a disciple maker.* Encourage him to take everything that he has learned and give it to someone else! He should witness to others and teach them the basics of the Christian faith. With another copy of the same booklet you used, he could lead some other new or immature Christian to learn the foundational beliefs of the Christian faith.

Likewise, he should become an active participant in a local church ministry. He should dedicate himself to do whatever God wants. He should establish solid habits that help him grow as a Christian, including a regular time for personal Bible study. As you read the following section, place yourself in the shoes of a new Christian by imagining that you are hearing these truths for the first time.

Witnessing–Talking about God

What is a witness? A witness is one who has seen and heard something and has been called to testify about it before others.

61

Discussion

Goal: Learn inductively the New Testament directions for church services.

In this exercise, you will lead your students in considering several New Testament passages pertaining to church worship services in order to show them the biblical foundation for what Christians do in church. Though it could be a very in-depth study, this exercise shows the basic reasons that we conduct church services the way we do. Obviously, the details of services in each church differ slightly. Prepare carefully so that you can explain your particular situation to your students. If they are all from one church, you can deal very directly with the issue. If they are from different churches, you should gain information on the differences in their services before going into the exercise. This discussion is not intended to cause contention or doubt but to solidify students' confidence in the customs and procedures of the modern church.

Have students read these passages one category at a time:

1. *Meetings:* Acts 20:7-12; Hebrews 10:25

2. *Preaching:* Acts 5:42; 6:7; II Timothy 4:2

3. *Prayer:* Acts 2:42; James 5:16

Ask your class to think up some ways to get people involved in evangelism and discipleship activities. Bring up church and youth group witnessing programs, tract programs, and small-group Bible studies. Gather the students' thoughts about the spiritual value of these various activities; point out the benefits of these methods of outreach. Ask the students for other ideas on how to involve people in disciple making.

Ammunition for Witnessing
Your students need to memorize all of the verses and verse explanations on page 62 of the student text. The students should be able to help a lost person find and understand each verse.

One of the last things Jesus said before He ascended into heaven after His resurrection was, "Ye shall be witnesses" (Acts 1:8). The early church took this to heart, and Christianity grew rapidly.

The responsibility to be a witness for Christ is every bit as heavy upon us today as it was in the first century. You may feel that you have not studied the Bible enough to witness effectively, but if you are a Christian, you can at least give someone else the testimony of how you were saved. The blind man in John 9 did not know much about Jesus either, but he knew that he had been changed. He said to the Pharisees, "Whether he [Jesus] be a sinner or no, I know not: one thing I know, that, whereas I was blind, now I see" (v. 25).

That simple testimony is enough for a start, but you will need to become familiar with Bible verses that will lend authority to what you say. You will find some verses effective for evangelistic purposes in the back of this book. Insert these verses into your personal testimony as you witness. Become familiar with the brief explanation of each verse given below.

Romans 3:23	This verse means everyone has sinned. No one has measured up to God's standard of holiness.
Romans 6:23	Because of our sin we deserve to spend eternity separated from God in hell–eternal death.
Ephesians 2:8-9	There is nothing we can do to save ourselves. Salvation is a gift from God.
John 3:16	God's great love for us caused Him to send His Son to die in our place and suffer our hell for us.
John 1:12	We must believe Christ died for us and personally receive Him to have eternal life.
Isaiah 55:7	God expects that if a man truly desires to be saved, he will turn from sin at the same time he turns to God.

62

4. *Reading Scripture:* I Timothy 4:13; II Timothy 3:15-17

5. *Service:* I Corinthians 16:15-16; I Peter 4:10-11

6. *Teaching:* I Timothy 4:11; II Timothy 4:2

7. *Worship:* Ephesians 5:19-20; Hebrews 12:28

As you read the verses under each topic, point out what they teach us to do in Christian worship services; write the actions on the board. You may have a list that parallels the seven activities above, or you may analyze the passages differently.

Draw the connections between these verses and the regular practice of your church. Point out that the instructions are not overly detailed. Even though written long ago to a different culture, they can still be applied to our churches. The Lord gives many instructions for His churches, but He words these instructions in such a way that they apply to all Christians in all times throughout the centuries.

1. What does Jesus promise to give you that will encourage you as you witness (Matt. 28:20b)? **His personal presence**

2. What did the early church pray for (Acts 4:29)? **Boldness to speak the Word of God**

3. Why is it so important to keep your life clean (Matt. 5:16)? **So other people will "see your good works and glorify your Father which is in heaven"**

4. What are two results of leading someone to Christ (James 5:20)?

   a. **Saves a soul from death**
   b. **Hides a multitude of sins**

5. What does God say about the man who "wins souls" (tries to lead people to Christ) (Prov. 11:30b)? **He is wise.**

Begin reading good books on soulwinning and become active in your church visitation program. Take every opportunity that God gives to tell others what God has done for you.

For additional help on talking about God, study the personal witnessing of Christ in John 3 as He talked with Nicodemus and in John 4 as He talked with the woman at the well.

Church Attendance–Meeting with God's People

In Acts 2:42 the Bible says that the new Christians "continued stedfastly in the apostles' doctrine [solid biblical teaching] and fellowship." These two elements are essential to Christian growth. God has established the local church as the means to meet these needs. Some today would scorn meeting together in an organized fashion. It is true that some churches have nothing to offer the believer who is seeking to be fed from God's Word, but God has not abandoned this institution. Of course, a Christian must use caution in selecting the right kind of church. God has chosen to use the church to build up His people. As long as a church stands true to God's Word, God will bless it and protect it.

Jesus' Example
This is a good time for reviewing John 3 and 4, examined earlier in the text. You may ask your students to retrace how the Lord progressively revealed to Nicodemus and the woman the same truths elaborated by the six verses in this lesson. For example, John 3:3 and 3:5-7 artfully make the same points by implication that Romans 3:23, Romans 6:23, and Ephesians 2:8-9 state plainly.

Exercise
Have each student write and turn in an explanation of how a new convert goes about joining his church. Students may need to talk to their pastors or other church leaders. The paper should be from one-half page to a whole page in length. Grade it according to clarity (and accuracy, if possible).

Discussion: Attending a Good Church
Goal: Advise your students how to steer a new convert toward a good church.

Procedure: Ask your students to discuss the following scenario.

"After leading Tim to Christ, you start meeting him once a week for discipleship lessons (you call them 'Bible studies' so Tim doesn't think you are condescending to him). Though you have invited him to your church, Tim starts going to a church that does not believe the Bible or preach the gospel. Tim does not see these problems. He likes the church because he has friends who go there and the services are fun. What action do you take, if any?"

Gather feedback from your students about this situation. Have them consider the danger of insulting Tim as well as the danger of letting Tim fall

The Pastor and His People

The progression of ideas in Ephesians 4:12 is this: the pastor perfects the saints, the saints do the work of the ministry, and the saints' work leads to the edification of the body of Christ. To "perfect" the saints is to equip them for service or teach them what a Christian should know and do.

The pastor teaches his people how to do the work of the ministry, and then they do it. The "work of the ministry" is "edifying" (strengthening and enlarging) the "body of Christ," the church. Thus, it is God's plan for pastors to equip Christians to work in the ministry and then for the Christians to build up the church by teaching, witnessing, discipling, serving, encouraging, and so forth.

Concern without Compromise

The point of Proverbs 4:14 is to avoid participating in the activities of ungodly friends. The term *way* refers to the course and activity of people's lives. However, the verse does not mean you should shun unsaved friends to the point that you cannot witness to them. Reach out to lost people but avoid participating in their sins.

1. According to Ephesians 4:11, God has set up certain types of Christian workers. One of these is the pastor. Verse 12 expresses the reason for his work. What is his purpose? **Perfecting the saints**

2. What is the pastor's responsibility according to Acts 20:28? **Oversee and feed the flock of God**

3. Some of the early believers in New Testament times had a certain problem. What was it (Heb. 10:25)? **They stopped meeting with other Christians.**

4. As Acts 2:42 points out, "fellowship" is essential to Christian growth. What benefit of fellowship does Ecclesiastes 4:9-10 describe? **Mutual support in difficult times**

5. What is another benefit of Christian fellowship (Heb. 10:24)? **We gain opportunities to stir other Christians to greater love and greater works.**

6. What is the proper attitude toward church (Ps. 122:1)? **Gladness, joy, and appreciation**

7. In contrast to fellowship with Christians, what is to be our response to ungodly friends (Prov. 4:14)? **Stay away from them.**

8. Proverbs 13:20 says "He that walketh with wise men shall be wise." What does the rest of this verse say is the end of the man who does not seek Christian fellowship? **He will be destroyed.**

Although it is important to attend church, a young believer must be selective in the church he attends. The Bible gives definite instructions as to the kind of church a Christian should fellowship with.

Matthew 28:19-20—Its members must be concerned about reaching the unsaved for Christ both at home and around the world.

I Corinthians 15:3-4—It must have the gospel as its central message. This means its pastor and teachers will continually be telling their listeners how to be saved. They will offer regular times of "invitation" when a person can get help on how to be saved.

64

under ungodly influences. You need to provide solutions based on your own judgment, but here is one approach you might suggest: Be patient about confronting Tim directly on the matter, but focus on lessons in your Bible studies that teach the truth about doctrines that his church fails to teach or apply correctly. For example, teach him carefully what the gospel really is so that he will recognize a false gospel on his own. If he persists in attending the wrong church, you will need to challenge him about his compromising behavior. Do not sever your friendship with him but make it clear that he is disobeying the God he claims to believe.

I Timothy 3:1-13—Its leaders should meet God's qualifications of dedication and holy living.

II Corinthians 6:14, 17—It should be independent of ungodly alliances and associations with religious organizations that do not obey the Bible or that do not hold it to be entirely true (inerrant).

Churches that meet these qualifications often describe themselves as "independent," "fundamental," and "evangelistic." Once you have found the right church, get involved in the soulwinning activities and attend all the services. God has raised up churches such as these to strengthen you spiritually through biblical preaching and teaching and through fellowship with other believers who love and obey the Bible as you do.

Dedication–Surrendering to God's Will

Once you repent of your sin and accept Jesus Christ as your Savior, you should soon realize that you are not your own. You belong to God. The apostle Paul said it this way:

> "What? know ye not that your body is the temple of the Holy Ghost which is in you, which ye have of God, and ye are not your own? For ye are bought with a price: therefore glorify God in your body, and in your spirit, which are God's."

> I Corinthians 6:19-20

According to I Peter 1:18-19, what are we purchased with?
The precious blood of Christ

In Romans 12:1, Paul states that God wants us to present (give over) our bodies as a living sacrifice to Him. The picture Paul portrays here brings to mind the Old Testament sacrifices where an animal was killed and offered to God. Paul is saying that we are to be dead (sacrificed), yet "living." We are to be alive physically, yet we are to consider ourselves dead to our flesh (our sinful nature). Romans 6:11 teaches this idea as well.

> "Likewise reckon [consider] ye also yourselves to be dead indeed unto sin, but alive unto God through Jesus Christ our Lord."

65

Reinforcement

On the subject of dedication, it is vital that the students do not misunderstand the nature of this decision. It is not limited to a single moment in the way salvation is. Dedication over a lifetime is a series of conscious choices to do God's will.

If a student has never deliberately told God that he will do whatever God wants, he should. He does not have to give a public testimony about his decision; he can keep it a private matter between himself and the Lord.

Though it could be impractical in your situation, this is an excellent time to deal with students one-on-one about their personal dedication. Especially try to take time with the more spiritually minded students in your class; you can usually help them more than resistant students.

God wants you to allow Him to totally control your body. He also wants to control what you do with your life since He owns you.

If you have not done so before, now would be a good time to bow your head and tell God that you want Him to have full control of you from this time on—you are now presenting your body to Him as a "living sacrifice." Also, tell Him you recognize that since He bought you, He owns you; thus, you will do anything He wants you to do. This decision is called dedication.

After you have decided to surrender your body and life to God in this way, you will want to ask yourself, "What does God want me to do with my life now?" Several considerations are suggested for you below.

A. Ask yourself, "What can I do for Christ now?"

1. List the opportunities in your church where you may be able to serve (helping with the youth program, visiting shut-ins, driving a bus, and so forth).
2. List the abilities, skills, and talents that you have that can be used for God now.
3. In what ways can you be a testimony for Christ? At home? At work? At school?

B. Ask yourself, "What can I do for Christ in the future?"

1. Has God placed on your heart a burden for a particular type of work or Christian service? If so, what is it?
2. Are you willing to serve God anywhere?
3. Do you need additional educational preparation?

Note: Often someone who has recently been saved finds it helpful to prepare for service at a Christian school. If you think this might be what the Lord has for you, write to the address on page 24 and ask for information on obtaining Christian education.

In Proverbs 3:5-6 God promises to "direct your paths" if you "acknowledge him in all your ways." God bless you as you seek to find and do His will.

For additional help about surrendering to God's will, see Luke 9:23-26.

Complete Consecration
Luke 9:23-26 begins, "If any man will come after me, let him deny himself, and take up his cross daily, and follow me." It continues by exposing the worthlessness of worldly gain when the soul is lost. It also warns against the danger of being ashamed of Christ.

Additional Helps for Christian Growth

A Plan for a Daily Quiet Time with God

Nothing will help you grow more and build your relationship with God more quickly than a daily quiet time. This is a time when you meet with God. Remember the following points as you begin to make this a part of your schedule.

1. Establish a regular time. Many Christians find that early morning is best since meeting with God early ensures that their first thoughts will be of spiritual things (Ps. 5:3).

2. Get alone. Shut yourself up in a room away from the distractions of people (Matt. 6:6).

3. Have a pen and notebook ready. Proverbs 10:14*a* says, "Wise men lay [store] up knowledge." Be ready to write down anything that God points out to you from His Word.

You should include the following elements in your quiet time:

A. Bible Reading

   Pray before you begin reading. Ask God to show you something just for yourself (Ps. 119:18).

   Follow a Bible reading schedule so that your reading is not haphazard. Some find that including the chapter of Proverbs that corresponds to the day of the month is helpful too. For example, read Proverbs 15 on the fifteenth day of the month, and so on.

   Read until God points out something especially for you. Jot down the verse and your immediate thoughts about it. As you read, God will convict you of sins in your life. Write down your decision to forsake these sins. Confess these to God and ask for power to overcome them in your prayer time. God uses His Word to cleanse us (John 15:3).

Thank God for what He has shown you in your reading.

Share these special verses and insights with others (I John 1:3).

B. Meditation—4M Formula

Mark verses in your Bible from the "Verses for Victory" section or from your own Bible reading, and write them out on cards to carry with you.

Memorize these verses in free moments during the day (Ps. 119:11).

Meditate on one verse or passage for a few minutes during your quiet time (Ps. 1:2-3). In meditation you are thinking of applications of these verses to your life. You are "personalizing" God's Word.

Master these Bible truths in your daily life. God will bring opportunities into your life for you to "exercise" and grow stronger (Heb. 5:14).

C. Prayer—Keeping a Personal Prayer Journal

Our prayers to God should contain a balance of praise, confession, thanksgiving, and supplication (asking). You can keep this balance by letting the little word "ACT" remind you of these elements. Begin your daily prayer time by "ACTing." Memorize the Scripture passages following each element and pray them back to God from the depths of your heart.

Adoring God for who He is (Ps. 8; I Chron. 29:11-13)

Confessing your sin (I John 1:9; Ps. 32:1-5)

Thanking Him for what He has done (Ps. 100:4)

Then, you may ask God to act. This is the time when you "let your requests be made known unto God" (Phil. 4:6).

A balanced prayer life has times of fellowship with God (this is when you "ACT") and times of petition to God for help. Our tendency is to forget the times of adoration and thanksgiving. Without them, however, our prayer life becomes a shallow "give me" time. Your times of adoration and thanksgiving will become easier as you see God answer your requests. Of course, this does not mean that every time you pray you must include all four elements, but none of them should be missing from your regular prayer life. If you wish, use the Personal Prayer Journal in the supplement to help you get started. A Bible Reading Schedule for the New Testament is on the reverse side of the Prayer Journal. This reading schedule will help keep you consistent. If you are a new Christian, begin by reading I John, the Gospel of John, and James; then go back and finish the rest of the New Testament. Write the date you read the passage in the box in front of the day's assignment. After you have read the entire New Testament, secure a schedule for the whole Bible and read the Bible through yearly.

Verses for Victory

Forgiveness	I John 1:9	Ps. 103:12	I John 2:1-2
Patience	Heb. 10:36	James 1:2-4	I Pet. 2:20
Strength	Eph. 3:16	Phil. 4:13	Eph. 6:10-11
Lust (1)	II Tim. 2:22	I John 2:15-17	I Pet. 2:11
Lust (2)	Matt. 5:28	Rom. 13:14	James 1:15
Priorities	Matt. 6:33	Acts 20:24	Phil. 3:8
Self-Discipline	Eccl. 5:4	Luke 9:23	James 1:19-20
Pleasing God	Matt. 6:24	Eph. 6:6-7	Col. 3:23
Christian Walk	Eph. 4:1-2	Eph. 5:2	Eph. 5:8-9
Temptation	I Cor. 10:13	James 4:7	Rom. 6:11-13
Peace	John 14:27	John 16:33	Phil. 4:6-7
Wise Counsel	Prov. 11:14	Prov. 12:15	Prov. 1:5
Courage	Ps. 31:24	Ps. 34:4	Prov. 29:25
Pride (1)	Prov. 16:18	Rom. 12:3	James 4:6
Pride (2)	Obad. 1:4	Matt. 20:26-27	I Cor. 4:7
Love	Deut. 6:5	John 13:35	John 15:13
Worldliness	Rom. 12:2	Col. 3:2	James 4:4
Tongue	James 3:6	Eph. 4:29	Prov. 10:19
Lying	Ps. 120:2	Ps. 101:7	Prov. 19:5
Stealing	Eph. 4:28	Prov. 30:8-9	Exod. 20:15
Suffering	Rom. 8:18	Phil. 1:29	I Pet. 2:21
Church Attendance	Ps. 122:1	Matt. 18:20	Heb. 10:25
Evil Thoughts	II Cor. 10:5	Phil. 4:8	Eph. 5:12
Critical Spirit	I Cor. 10:10	Phil. 2:14	James 5:9
Strong Drink	Isa. 5:11	Hab. 2:15	Rom. 14:21
Guidance	Prov. 3:5-6	Ps. 32:8	Prov. 1:23
Forgiving Others	Matt. 5:44	Mark 11:25	Eph. 4:32
Knowing God	Jer. 9:23-24	John 17:3	Phil. 3:8-10
Assurance	John 3:36	John 10:28	I John 5:13

As you find other areas of need and Verses for Victory, write them in the space below.

Personal Prayer Journal

Include these elements in your regular prayer time.

I. Include a time when you "ACT."

Adoring God for who He is (Ps. 8; I Chron. 29:11-13)

Confessing your sin (I John 1:9; Ps. 32:1-5)

Thanking Him for what He has done (Ps. 100:4)

II. Include a time when you ask God to "act" (Phil. 4:6).
(Write these requests in the spaces below.)

Date Requested	Request	Date Answered

Memory Verses

1. Assurance

   "He that believeth on the Son hath everlasting life: and he that believeth not the Son shall not see life; but the wrath of God abideth on him." John 3:36

2. Assurance

   "And I give unto them eternal life; and they shall never perish, neither shall any man pluck them out of my hand." John 10:28

3. We are all sinners

   "For all have sinned, and come short of the glory of God." Romans 3:23

4. The penalty of sin

   "For the wages of sin is death; but the gift of God is eternal life through Jesus Christ our Lord." Romans 6:23

5. We cannot save ourselves

   "For by grace are ye saved through faith; and that not of yourselves: it is the gift of God: Not of works, lest any man should boast." Ephesians 2:8-9

6. Christ died for us

   "For God so loved the world, that he gave his only begotten Son, that whosoever believeth in him should not perish, but have everlasting life." John 3:16

7. We must believe on Christ

   "But as many as received him, to them gave he power to become the sons of God, even to them that believe on his name." John 1:12

8. We must turn from sin

   "Let the wicked forsake his way, and the unrighteous man his thoughts: and let him return unto the Lord, and he will have mercy upon him; and to our God, for he will abundantly pardon." Isaiah 55:7

Review Questions

True or False

_F_ 1. God's promises to answer our prayers are unconditional.

_T_ 2. I Corinthians 6:19-20 implies a person can be saved but not be glorifying God with his body.

Short/Long Answer

3. What verse from the section "Prayer—Talking With God" in Chapter 4 does a disciple who says "God just doesn't seem real to me" need to understand and believe?

   James 4:8

4. Remembering Chapter 1 of this book, which verse from "Witnessing" will be the hardest for your disciple to get unsaved people to believe? Why?

   Romans 6:23—sinners hate to hear that they are so bad they deserve hell.

5. According to the questions in "Church Attendance," list five benefits a new convert will receive from a good church. Include the Scripture references.

   1. Guidance of a pastor (Eph. 4:11)

   2. Protection of a pastor (Acts 20:28)

   3. Support in hard times (Eccl. 4:9-10)

   4. Help in loving others and doing good works (Heb. 10:24)

   5. Wisdom (Prov. 13:20)

__A__ 6. What is the best way for a new convert with little Bible knowledge to witness to others?

   A. Sharing his personal testimony
   B. Passing out tracts
   C. Preaching on street corners
   D. Waiting to witness until he learns more about the Bible.

__C__ 7. Which of the following comments from a new believer would most likely indicate that the church he attends does not meet the qualifications set down in "Church Attendance"?

   A. "It seems like every month there is another sermon on how to get saved!" (see I Corinthians 15:3-4)
   B. "Those people seem totally preoccupied with witnessing!" (see Matthew 28:19-20)
   C. "The pastor told me that the Bible never says anything about drinking!" (see I Timothy 3:1-13)
   D. None of these

8. Explain in your own words what gives God the right to tell you what to do with your whole life.

   Key ideas: God created me, so He owns me. Christ took all the penalty for my sin, so He is responsible for my new life on earth. God gives me the power to do His will, so nothing He demands is unreasonable.

9-10. Suppose someone you are discipling shows you this prayer journal after his first week of regular devotions. Write one thing to praise him for and two problems you see that he needs to work on.

Date	Bible	Application	Request	Answer
4/6	Prov 6	A proud look is wrong	Help me find a better job	Yes
4/7	Prov 7	Prostitution is evil	Help me find a good mechanic	Didn't
4/8	Prov 8	Wisdom is important	Show me if I should quit this job.	
4/9	Prov 9	Don't correct a mocker	Good weather this Saturday	No
4/10	Prov 10	Don't talk too much	Get my boss to leave	

Suggestions: Good! You were consistent, and you followed a systematic pattern, reading a different chapter from Proverbs each day. But look at your applications; they are too general and not personal; they need to address things you need to change. Likewise, most prayer requests should be for your own spiritual growth or others' needs. Do you see how your requests almost sound selfish?

75

Notes

Notes

Appendix A

John 3

Prologue:

A man of the Pharisees named Nicodemus, a ruler of the Jews, came to Jesus by night and said,

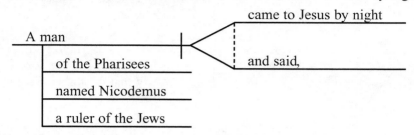

FIRST DIALOGUE

Nicodemus   Jesus

Rabbi,
we know you are a teacher from God

[because]

no man can do these miracles unless God is with him.

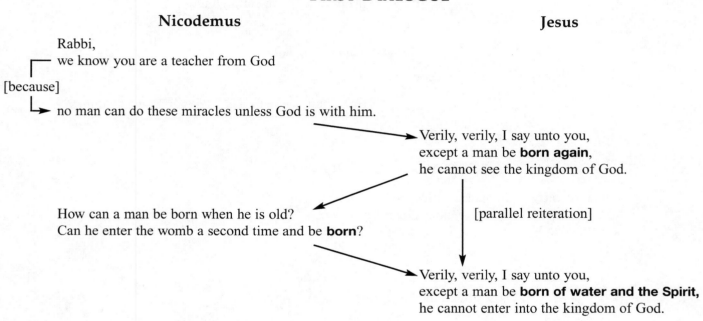

Verily, verily, I say unto you,
except a man be **born again**,
he cannot see the kingdom of God.

[parallel reiteration]

How can a man be born when he is old?
Can he enter the womb a second time and be **born**?

Verily, verily, I say unto you,
except a man be **born of water and the Spirit,**
he cannot enter into the kingdom of God.

FIRST EXPLANATION

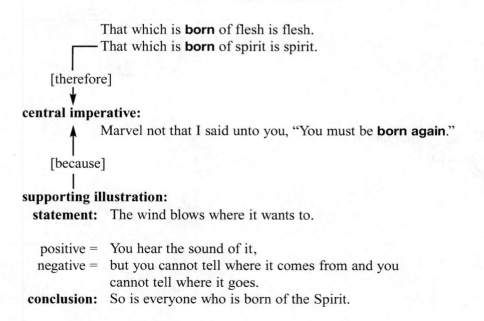

That which is **born** of flesh is flesh.
That which is **born** of spirit is spirit.

[therefore]

central imperative:
Marvel not that I said unto you, "You must be **born again**."

[because]

supporting illustration:
statement: The wind blows where it wants to.

positive = You hear the sound of it,
negative = but you cannot tell where it comes from and you
cannot tell where it goes.
conclusion: So is everyone who is born of the Spirit.

SECOND DIALOGUE

Nicodemus   **Jesus**

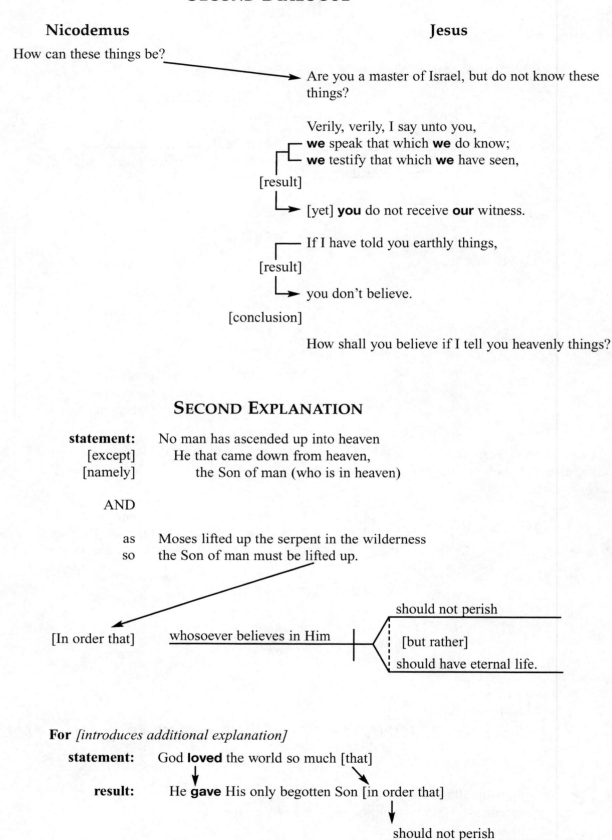

How can these things be?

Are you a master of Israel, but do not know these things?

Verily, verily, I say unto you,
- **we** speak that which **we** do know;
- **we** testify that which **we** have seen,

[result]

[yet] **you** do not receive **our** witness.

If I have told you earthly things,

[result]

you don't believe.

[conclusion]

How shall you believe if I tell you heavenly things?

SECOND EXPLANATION

statement: No man has ascended up into heaven
[except]   He that came down from heaven,
[namely]   the Son of man (who is in heaven)

AND

as   Moses lifted up the serpent in the wilderness
so   the Son of man must be lifted up.

[In order that]   whosoever believes in Him

should not perish
[but rather]
should have eternal life.

For *[introduces additional explanation]*

statement: God **loved** the world so much [that]

result: He **gave** His only begotten Son [in order that]

should not perish

purpose: whosoever believes in Him
[but rather]
should have eternal life.

For *[further explanation]*

    statement: God sent His Son into the world
    negative: not [in order to] condemn the world
    purpose: but [in order that] *the world through Him might be saved.*

Climax of narrative

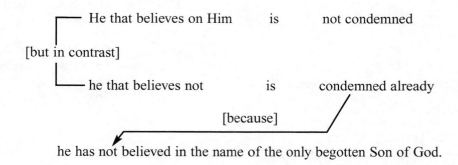

He that believes on Him   is   not condemned

[but in contrast]

he that believes not   is   condemned already

[because]

he has not believed in the name of the only begotten Son of God.

And *[clarifies reason for condemnation]*

    This is the condemnation:

    Light is come into the world,

    [but] **men loved darkness** rather than light

    [because] their deeds were evil.

For *[clarifies reason men love darkness]*

    Everyone that does evil

    hates the light,

    neither comes to the light,

    [lest] his deeds should be reproved.

But *[in contrast to one doing evil]*

    He that does truth

    comes to the Light

    [in order that] his deeds may be manifested

    [specifically] that they are wrought in God.

Appendix B

John 4

Begin in verse 7, skipping the explanatory note in verse 8.

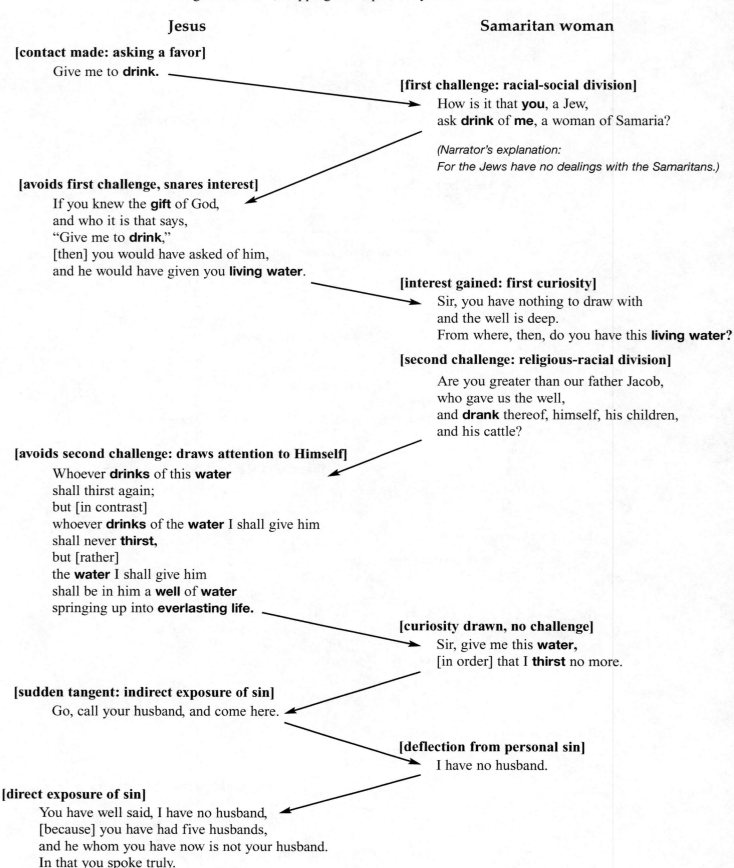

Jesus

[contact made: asking a favor]
Give me to **drink.**

[avoids first challenge, snares interest]
If you knew the **gift** of God,
and who it is that says,
"Give me to **drink**,"
[then] you would have asked of him,
and he would have given you **living water**.

[avoids second challenge: draws attention to Himself]
Whoever **drinks** of this **water**
shall thirst again;
but [in contrast]
whoever **drinks** of the **water** I shall give him
shall never **thirst,**
but [rather]
the **water** I shall give him
shall be in him a **well** of **water**
springing up into **everlasting life.**

[sudden tangent: indirect exposure of sin]
Go, call your husband, and come here.

[direct exposure of sin]
You have well said, I have no husband,
[because] you have had five husbands,
and he whom you have now is not your husband.
In that you spoke truly.

Samaritan woman

[first challenge: racial-social division]
How is it that **you**, a Jew,
ask **drink** of **me**, a woman of Samaria?

(Narrator's explanation:
For the Jews have no dealings with the Samaritans.)

[interest gained: first curiosity]
Sir, you have nothing to draw with
and the well is deep.
From where, then, do you have this **living water?**

[second challenge: religious-racial division]
Are you greater than our father Jacob,
who gave us the well,
and **drank** thereof, himself, his children,
and his cattle?

[curiosity drawn, no challenge]
Sir, give me this **water,**
[in order] that I **thirst** no more.

[deflection from personal sin]
I have no husband.

Jesus
Samaritan woman

**[second deflection from sin with third challenge:
racial-religious]**

> Sir, I perceive that you are a **prophet**.
> Our fathers **worshiped** in this mountain,
> [but] you say that Jerusalem
> is the place where people should **worship**.

**[avoids third challenge: reveals weakness
of worldly religion and the nature of true religion]**

> Woman, believe me,
> the hour is coming when you shall
> neither in this mountain nor at Jerusalem
> **worship** the Father.
>
> You do not know what you **worship**.
> [In contrast] we know what we **worship**
> [because] **salvation** is of the Jews.
> [However]
> the hour is coming, and now is, when

central declaration:

> the true **worshipers** shall **worship** the Father
> in Spirit and in truth,
> [because] the Father is seeking such people
> to **worship** Him.

[further explanation of the central declaration]

> God is **spirit**;
> [therefore] they that **worship** Him
> must **worship** Him
> in **spirit** and in **truth.**

**[final deflection: sensing a personal call,
she tries one more evasion]**

> I know that **Messiah** comes,
> who is called **Christ**.
> When **He** comes,
> **He** will tell us all things.

**[CLIMAX: demands a personal decision to believe
or reject]**

> **I** that speaketh unto you am **He.**

Hark, the Voice of Jesus Calling

Daniel March, 1816-1909

Ascribed to Wolfgang A. Mozart, 1756-1791
Arr. by Hubert P. Main, 1839-1925

1. Hark, the voice of Je-sus call-ing, "Who will go and work to-day?
2. If you can-not cross the o-cean And the heath-en lands ex-plore,
3. Let none hear you i-dly say-ing, "There is noth-ing I can do,"

Fields are white, and har-vests wait-ing, Who will bear the sheaves a-way?"
You can find the heath-en near-er, You can help them at your door:
While the souls of men are dy-ing, And the Mas-ter calls for you:

Loud and long the Mas-ter call-eth, Rich re-ward He of-fers thee;
If you can-not give your thou-sands, You can give the wid-ow's mite;
Glad-ly take the task He gives you; Let His work your pleas-ure be;

Who will an-swer, glad-ly say-ing, "Here am I; send me, send me"?
And the least you give for Je-sus Will be pre-cious in His sight.
An-swer quick-ly when He call-eth, "Here am I; send me, send me."

TEST ONE

Memory Verses

Write the following verses on your own paper.

1-3. Matthew 28:18-20

4-5. Acts 1:8

6-8. Luke 24:45-48

True or False

_____ 9. Britain in the eighteenth century was mostly made up of nominal Christians.

_____ 10. In Ezekiel's vision, the wheels and living creatures represent earthly kingdoms fighting for control of the world.

_____ 11. Ezekiel could not have disobeyed God even if he had wanted to.

_____ 12. Christ taught that hell lasts forever and that people in hell suffer consciously.

_____ 13. It is good to be aggressive when witnessing for Christ.

_____ 14. Nicodemus had no way of knowing Jesus was the Messiah until Jesus told him so.

_____ 15. A major theme in the three parables about lost things is rejoicing.

Short Answer

16. The first British missionary in the modern missionary movement was_____.

17-18. Suppose you are the messenger God sends to warn certain people to repent of their sins. However, you refuse to obey God and do not warn them about God's judgment. What will happen to them and to you?

  A. Them:_____

  B. You:_____

  _____

19. What passage was the Ethiopian reading when Philip approached his chariot?_____

20-21. List two spiritual realities pictured by baptism._____

_____

22. What does the word "teaching" mean in the Great Commission? _____

_____

_____

23. What is the most prominent tool of God's judgment in the Old Testament?_____

Terms

24. The Bible's word for "the inner person encompassing your thinking, feeling, and decision making"

is the_____.

25. "Going out of set bounds into an off-limits area" is_____.

26. "The one-time sign of commitment, transformation, change of direction, and the start of a new

life" is_____.

Multiple Choice

_____ 27. What is the best description of sin?
   A. Ignorance of God's will that leads to foolish words and actions
   B. Missing the intended target
   C. Taking a wrong turn somewhere in life
   D. Actively going in a direction other than the direction God commands
   E. Stubbornly refusing to follow God's direct orders

_____ 28. Which of the following is an improper definition of justification?
   A. To pronounce, accept, and treat as just
   B. To progressively make holy through faith and good works
   C. To declare legally not guilty of crime and therefore not deserving of punishment
   D. To reckon the righteousness of Christ to belong to a sinner
   E. To consider a person to have the full status and privileges of one who has kept the law

_____ 29. Which of the following is not a legitimate kind of sanctification?
   A. Being set apart from the world at the moment of salvation
   B. Growing steadily more like Christ after salvation
   C. Avoiding wicked people as sensitivity to sin increases
   D. Final separation from sin in heaven
   E. All of these are legitimate kinds of sanctification.

_____ 30. According to the text, which of these ideas is not taught by the Parable of the Lost Coin?
   A. Persistence
   B. Preoccupation with the lost thing
   C. Compassion

_____ 31. According to Christ, about how many of all the people we witness to will be saved?
   A. 25%
   B. 50%
   C. 75%
   D. None of these

Essay

32-33. Why was the Lord's Great Commission so startling in the ancient Roman world?_____

_____

_____

_____

_____

_____

34-36. Suppose someone you know does not believe God sends people to the lake of fire forever.

Write a short paragraph summarizing what you should tell him, including the reason God

punishes people and at least one appropriate Scripture reference._____

_____

_____

_____

_____

_____

37-38. In His conversation with the Samaritan woman, what point was the Lord making when He

said that God is spirit?_____

_____

_____

_____

_____

Listing

39-42. List the five reasons witnessing is highly important. The first one is provided for you.

A. Christ came to seek and save the lost.

B. _____

C. _____

D. _____

E. _____

Matching

43-48. Match each type of response from the Parable of the Sower to its description below:

1. the way side   2. the stony ground   3. the thorny ground   4. the good ground

_____ A. The hearer refuses to believe the word when he hears it.

_____ B. The hearer is born again.

_____ C. The hearer has an impulsive response that does not last.

_____ D. The hearer produces abundant fruit.

_____ E. The hearer could be a carnal Christian or a lost man; it is difficult to know for sure.

_____ F. The hearer is kept from bearing fruit by sinful influences in the world.

Recall

49. What natural illustration and play on words did the Lord use to teach Nicodemus about the

Holy Spirit?_____

50. What natural illustration with a double meaning did the Lord use to teach the Samaritan

woman about eternal life?_____

ANSWERS—TEST ONE

Memory Verses

Write the following verses on your own paper.

1-3. Matthew 28:18-20

4-5. Acts 1:8

6-8. Luke 24:45-48

True or False

___T___   9. Britain in the eighteenth century was mostly made up of nominal Christians.

___F___ 10. In Ezekiel's vision, the wheels and living creatures represent earthly kingdoms fighting for control of the world.

___F___ 11. Ezekiel could not have disobeyed God even if he had wanted to.

___T___ 12. Christ taught that hell lasts forever and that people in hell suffer consciously.

___T___ 13. It is good to be aggressive when witnessing for Christ.

___F___ 14. Nicodemus had no way of knowing Jesus was the Messiah until Jesus told him so.

___T___ 15. A major theme in the three parables about lost things is rejoicing.

Short Answer

16. The first British missionary in the modern missionary movement was ___**William Carey**___.

17-18. Suppose you are the messenger God sends to warn certain people to repent of their sins. However, you refuse to obey God and do not warn them about God's judgment. What will happen to them and to you?

    A. Them: ___**They will perish because of their own sins.**___

    B. You: ___**God will require their blood at your hands. (You are held accountable for your disobedience.)**___

19. What passage was the Ethiopian reading when Philip approached his chariot? ___**Isaiah 53**___

20-21. List two spiritual realities pictured by baptism. ___**purification and union with Christ**___

22. What does the word "teaching" mean in the Great Commission? ___*deliberate, systematic*___

*instruction in everything Christ taught*_____

_____

23. What is the most prominent tool of God's judgment in the Old Testament?_____*fire*_____

Terms

24. The Bible's word for "the inner person encompassing your thinking, feeling, and decision making"

is the_____*heart*_____.

25. "Going out of set bounds into an off-limits area" is_____*transgression*_____.

26. "The one-time sign of commitment, transformation, change of direction, and the start of a new

life" is_____*baptism*_____.

Multiple Choice

___D___ 27. What is the best description of sin?
- A. Ignorance of God's will that leads to foolish words and actions
- B. Missing the intended target
- C. Taking a wrong turn somewhere in life
- D. Actively going in a direction other than the direction God commands
- E. Stubbornly refusing to follow God's direct orders

___B___ 28. Which of the following is an improper definition of justification?
- A. To pronounce, accept, and treat as just
- B. To progressively make holy through faith and good works
- C. To declare legally not guilty of crime and therefore not deserving of punishment
- D. To reckon the righteousness of Christ to belong to a sinner
- E. To consider a person to have the full status and privileges of one who has kept the law

___C___ 29. Which of the following is not a legitimate kind of sanctification?
- A. Being set apart from the world at the moment of salvation
- B. Growing steadily more like Christ after salvation
- C. Avoiding wicked people as sensitivity to sin increases
- D. Final separation from sin in heaven
- E. All of these are legitimate kinds of sanctification.

___C___ 30. According to the text, which of these ideas is not taught by the Parable of the Lost Coin?
- A. Persistence
- B. Preoccupation with the lost thing
- C. Compassion

<u>**D**</u>   31. According to Christ, about how many of all the people we witness to will be saved?
      A. 25%
      B. 50%
      C. 75%
      D. None of these

Essay

32-33. Why was the Lord's Great Commission so startling in the ancient Roman world?_____

Sample answer: Religion was very much a racial or regional characteristic. The

Romans did not consider any one god absolutely superior but simply placed all

gods into their pantheon. No one thought of one god as having all authority

and deserving everyone's worship.

34-36. Suppose someone you know does not believe God sends people to the lake of fire forever.

Write a short paragraph summarizing what you should tell him, including the reason God

punishes people and at least one appropriate Scripture reference. *God punishes people*

because of their sins. Romans 8:5-8 shows that it is impossible for an unsaved man

to do anything truly pleasing to God. Though God has done everything necessary

to save everyone who believes, humans still rebel against Him and refuse to accept

His salvation. Revelation 20 makes it clear that everyone who dies unsaved will go

to the lake of fire forever.

37-38. In His conversation with the Samaritan woman, what point was the Lord making when He

said that God is spirit? *Neither Mt. Gerizim in Samaria nor the Jerusalem temple*

was the only place to worship God because He is not limited to any one place. As

a spirit-being, He is present everywhere at once.

Listing

39-42. List the five reasons witnessing is highly important. The first one is provided for you.

A. Christ came to seek and save the lost.

B. *Christ commanded His disciples to reach the lost.*

C. *Christ sent the Holy Spirit to empower believers to reach the lost.*

D. *Christ expects us to witness as part of our worship to Him.*

E. *Christ views witnessing as evidence of the genuineness of our salvation.*

Matching

43-48. Match each type of response from the Parable of the Sower to its description below:

1. the way side 2. the stony ground 3. the thorny ground 4. the good ground

___1___ A. The hearer refuses to believe the word when he hears it.

___4___ B. The hearer is born again.

___2___ C. The hearer has an impulsive response that does not last.

___4___ D. The hearer produces abundant fruit.

___3___ E. The hearer could be a carnal Christian or a lost man; it is difficult to know for sure.

___3___ F. The hearer is kept from bearing fruit by sinful influences in the world.

Recall

49. What natural illustration and play on words did the Lord use to teach Nicodemus about the

Holy Spirit?_____ *wind (same as "spirit" in Greek)*_____

50. What natural illustration with a double meaning did the Lord use to teach the Samaritan

woman about eternal life?_____ *water ("living" water)*_____

TEST TWO

Memory Verses

Write the following verses on your own paper.

1-4. Ephesians 4:11-13

5-6. John 15:16

7-8. Colossians 1:28

Fill in the Blank

9-18.   Complete the outline below.

  I. Who is God?

    A. He is_____.

    B. He is_____.

    C. He is_____.

  II. What is man's problem?

    A. Man is guilty because of his_____.

    B. Man is guilty because of his_____.

    C. Man is separated from God because of his sin.

  III. What has God done?

    A. Christ is the God-man.

    B. Christ has no_____.

    C. Christ bore our_____and their_____on the cross.

    D. Christ_____as proof of His victory over sin and death.

  IV. What must man do?

    A. Man must_____.

    B. Man must_____.

Multiple Choice

_____ 19. If someone is lacking assurance of his salvation, which of the following would be the best thing to say to him?
- A. Can't you remember being saved?
- B. Do you feel close to God?
- C. You need to devote extra time to Bible reading in order to expose sin in your life.
- D. You need to be trusting Jesus Christ now, whether you think you were saved before or not.

_____ 20. Which relationship is likely to involve the greatest rapport?
- A. An airplane pilot and his passengers
- B. A boy and his pet puppy
- C. A teacher and student
- D. A husband and wife

_____ 21. From the human point of view, what is the goal of a witnessing conversation?
- A. Bring the person to the point of making a decision.
- B. Get the person to agree to come to your church.
- C. Persuade the person to let you talk to him again.
- D. Find out the person's reasons for not being saved.

_____ 22. Which of these is "the primary command of the Great Commission"?
- A. Go!
- B. Teach!
- C. Baptize!

_____ 23. Which of the following was not a feature of the early church worship services?
- A. Preaching
- B. Teaching
- C. Bible reading
- D. Prayer
- E. All of these were features.

Short Answer

24-25. What are the two parts of disciple making?_____

26-27. Give the special term for the poetic form of Psalm 119 and define what that term means.

(Hint: it has to do with the Hebrew alphabet.)_____

_____

28. What is the best English synonym for the word *power* in Matthew 28:18?_____

29. What is the basis of every relationship, including our relationship with God?_____

30-32. List three reasons our prayers may not be answered._____

_____

_____

33-34. List two errors that can arise from an imbalanced evangelism and discipleship program.

_____

_____

_____

35-38. Write a paragraph contrasting the two people to whom Christ witnessed in John 3 and 4. Include at least five characteristics of each person that contrast with the other individual's characteristics. _____

_____

_____

_____

_____

_____

_____

_____

_____

_____

_____

True or False

_____ 39. Prayer is necessary to gain forgiveness of sin.

_____ 40. It is proper to say that after a person is saved a battle rages in him between the Holy Spirit's guidance and Satan's temptation.

_____ 41. Praying for specific people to be saved is unnecessary because God wants everyone to be saved.

_____ 42. Personal evangelism is a purely divine endeavor.

_____ 43. Ezekiel had no reason to believe that any of the Jews would repent of their sin.

_____ 44. The prophet Ezekiel gives the most vivid Old Testament images of eternal punishment.

Matching

45-50. Match the verse reference with the content description below.

Romans 3:23   Romans 6:23   Ephesians 2:8-9   John 3:16   John 1:12   Isaiah 55:7

A. We must believe Christ died for us and personally receive Him to have eternal life.

_____

B. God's great love for us caused Him to send His Son to die in our place and suffer our punishment for us. _____

C. Everyone has sinned. No one has measured up to God's standard of holiness.

_____

D. God expects that if a man truly desires to be saved, he will turn from sin at the same time he turns to God. _____

E. Because of our sin we deserve to spend eternity separated from God in hell, the place of eternal death. _____

F. There is nothing we can do to save ourselves. Salvation is a gift from God.

_____

ANSWERS—TEST TWO

Memory Verses

Write the following verses on your own paper.

1-4. Ephesians 4:11-13

5-6. John 15:16

7-8. Colossians 1:28

Fill in the Blank

9-18.　Complete the outline below.

I. Who is God?

A. He is _____*loving*_____ .

B. He is _____*just*_____ .

C. He is _____*Lord over all*_____ .

II. What is man's problem?

A. Man is guilty because of his _____*sin nature*_____ .

B. Man is guilty because of his _____*sinful acts*_____ .

C. Man is separated from God because of his sin.

III. What has God done?

A. Christ is the God-man.

B. Christ has no _____*sin*_____ .

C. Christ bore our _____*sins*_____ and their _____*penalty*_____ on the cross.

D. Christ _____*rose from the grave*_____ as proof of His victory over sin and death.

IV. What must man do?

A. Man must _____*turn from his sin*_____ .

B. Man must _____*place his confidence in Christ*_____ .

Multiple Choice

__D__ 19. If someone is lacking assurance of his salvation, which of the following would be the best thing to say to him?
  A. Can't you remember being saved?
  B. Do you feel close to God?
  C. You need to devote extra time to Bible reading in order to expose sin in your life.
  D. You need to be trusting Jesus Christ now, whether you think you were saved before or not.

__D__ 20. Which relationship is likely to involve the greatest rapport?
  A. An airplane pilot and his passengers
  B. A boy and his pet puppy
  C. A teacher and student
  D. A husband and wife

__A__ 21. From the human point of view, what is the goal of a witnessing conversation?
  A. Bring the person to the point of making a decision.
  B. Get the person to agree to come to your church.
  C. Persuade the person to let you talk to him again.
  D. Find out the person's reasons for not being saved.

__B__ 22. Which of these is "the primary command of the Great Commission"?
  A. Go!   C. Baptize!
  B. Teach!

__E__ 23. Which of the following was not a feature of the early church worship services?
  A. Preaching   D. Prayer
  B. Teaching   E. All of these were features.
  C. Bible reading

Short Answer

24-25. What are the two parts of disciple making? **personal evangelism and discipleship**

26-27. Give the special term for the poetic form of Psalm 119 and define what that term means.

(Hint: it has to do with the Hebrew alphabet.) **acrostic—the first letters in the lines of each section are successive letters of the alphabet.**

28. What is the best English synonym for the word *power* in Matthew 28:18? **authority**

29. What is the basis of every relationship, including our relationship with God? **communication**

30-32. List three reasons our prayers may not be answered. **We ask amiss; our sins and iniquities hinder our prayers; we have not forgiven others. Also, God may have a secret, providential reason for not answering a prayer.**

33-34. List two errors that can arise from an imbalanced evangelism and discipleship program.

   1. Considering our responsibility at an end after a person gets saved

   2. Waiting passively for people to approach us on their own initiative to get

   saved and to learn about the Bible

35-38. Write a paragraph contrasting the two people to whom Christ witnessed in John 3 and 4. Include at least five characteristics of each person that contrast with the other individual's characteristics. *Sample answer: Nicodemus was a Jewish religious leader. He was politically prominent and probably wealthy. In contrast, the woman was a Samaritan who was not overtly religious. She appears to have been poor and politically insignificant. Nicodemus made no confession of faith, but the woman believed and immediately went to tell about Christ.*

_____

_____

_____

_____

_____

_____

True or False

__T__ 39. Prayer is necessary to gain forgiveness of sin.

__T__ 40. It is proper to say that after a person is saved a battle rages in him between the Holy Spirit's guidance and Satan's temptation.

__F__ 41. Praying for specific people to be saved is unnecessary because God wants everyone to be saved.

__F__ 42. Personal evangelism is a purely divine endeavor.

__T__ 43. Ezekiel had no reason to believe that any of the Jews would repent of their sin.

__F__ 44. The prophet Ezekiel gives the most vivid Old Testament images of eternal punishment.

Matching

45-50. Match the verse reference with the content description below.

Romans 3:23   Romans 6:23   Ephesians 2:8-9   John 3:16   John 1:12   Isaiah 55:7

A. We must believe Christ died for us and personally receive Him to have eternal life.
_____*John 1:12*_____

B. God's great love for us caused Him to send His Son to die in our place and suffer our punishment for us._____*John 3:16*_____

C. Everyone has sinned. No one has measured up to God's standard of holiness.
_____*Romans 3:23*_____

D. God expects that if a man truly desires to be saved, he will turn from sin at the same time he turns to God._____*Isaiah 55:7*_____

E. Because of our sin we deserve to spend eternity separated from God in hell, the place of eternal death._____*Romans 6:23*_____

F. There is nothing we can do to save ourselves. Salvation is a gift from God.
_____*Ephesians 2:8-9*_____